A Safe and Brave Space Anthology of Poetry and Art

By

Garden Sisters of the Garden of Neuro

Published by Garden of Neuro Publishing
Poughkeepsie, New York

October 2021

Library of Congress Control Number: 2021922152

ISBN 979-8-9851332-0-2 Paperback

Cover Art by: Katalina Gutierrez
Cover Design by: Val Maus
Edited by: Garden of Neuro Ambassadors
Internal Art: Garden of Neuro Members

Acknowledgements

We would like to acknowledge the following for their contributions to this publication:

Pratibha Savani, author of Tangles + Knots, for inspiring us to use black and white art for mindfulness colouring, in this anthology. And for editing the art contributions to this publication.

Katalina Gutierrez for creating and providing the cover art of the Chrysalis, watercolor on paper on the front cover and the Tree of Life, watercolor on board.

Anu Anniah for website consulting.

Val Maus for cover design.

To all the editors who volunteered their time to make this anthology shine, namely Shalu Ahuja, Nanci Arvizu, Lisa Bolin, Susan Brearley, Katalina Gutierrez, and Pratibha Savani.

Lisa Tomey, publishing guru and editor extraordinaire, for her mentorship, expertise, calm and caring demeanor, patience, and project management skills. She artfully curated and led workshops for women who made this entire anthology possible. She encouraged women who have never been published before, to deeply know in their core that they too were artists.

Dedication

This poetry anthology, the first of many to come from the women's collective that is found in the Garden of Neuro, is dedicated to all the women who nourished it, so that it could grow into what you hold in your hands. With grateful hearts for what we have birthed together, we share this with you dear reader, and invite you to be a part of this wonderful experiment that we have begun--a global women's community for honoring our differences as well as our shared experiences--for the benefit of all of us.

Safe and Brave Art Space

All artwork contributed by the Garden of Neuro Ambassadors

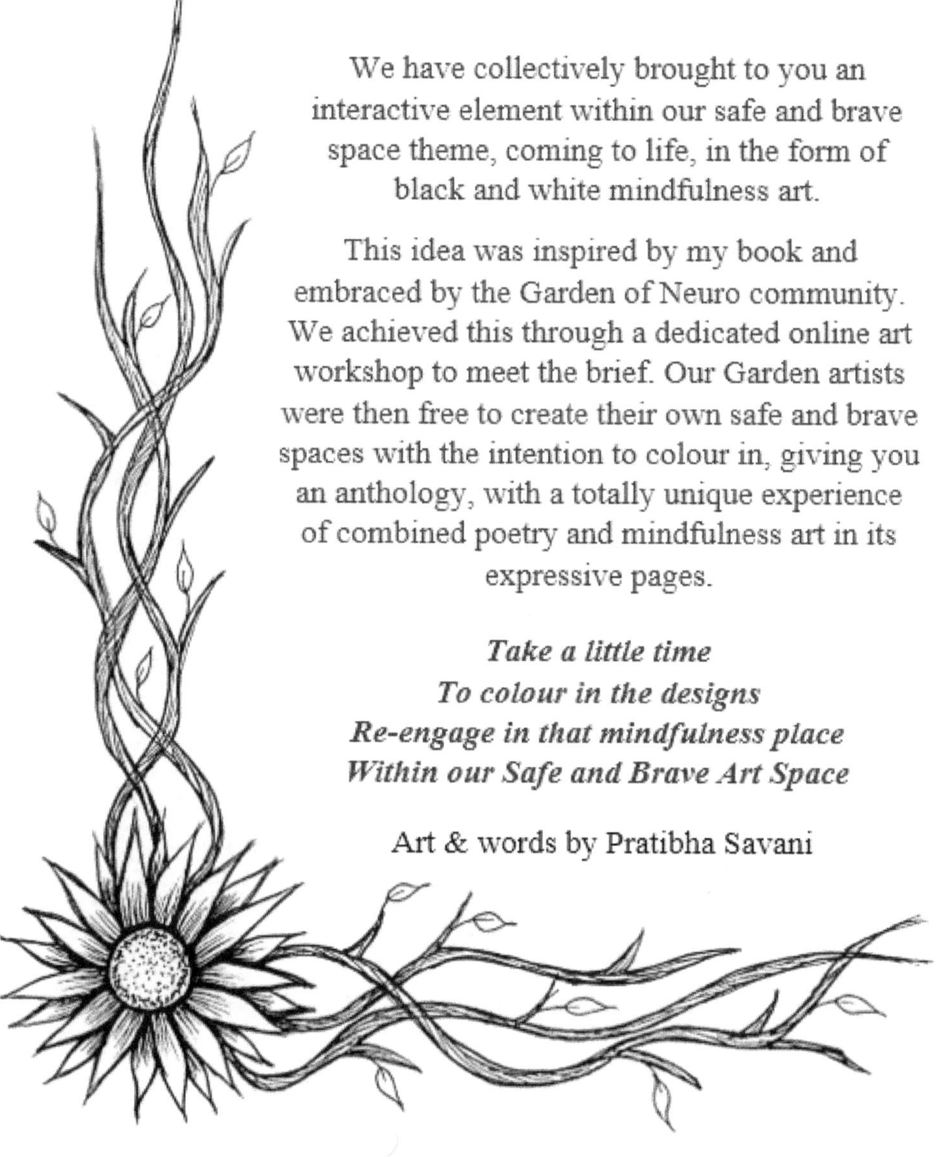

We have collectively brought to you an interactive element within our safe and brave space theme, coming to life, in the form of black and white mindfulness art.

This idea was inspired by my book and embraced by the Garden of Neuro community. We achieved this through a dedicated online art workshop to meet the brief. Our Garden artists were then free to create their own safe and brave spaces with the intention to colour in, giving you an anthology, with a totally unique experience of combined poetry and mindfulness art in its expressive pages.

Take a little time
To colour in the designs
Re-engage in that mindfulness place
Within our Safe and Brave Art Space

Art & words by Pratibha Savani

Welcome to Our Safe and Brave Space

Welcome to our #safe and brave space!
Where you can show your true face.
Leave all facades behind,
Place them gently upon the shelf.

Come explore our space,
no need to be relegated
to just one role,
no room for hyperbole!

We welcome you with open arms.
For in this space, trust is sacred.
We shall nurture your soul
like a sapling ready to soar.

In this family of women,
from across the globe,
we yearn to learn;
we embrace new knowledge!

Come check us out,
you'll be glad you did.
For here is a place so splendid!

Robin Klammer

Table of Contents

Susan Brearley

Susan Brearley is a brilliant strategist, a published book author, writer, seasoned editor, essayist, occasional comedy writer and EIC of MuddyUm, on Medium, and an accidental poet. She is currently based in the mid-Hudson Valley, New York, where she teaches haiku at Innisfree Garden in Millbrook. As the founder of the Garden of Neuro, you can find her there most any day.
Instagram: GardenofNeuro

The Garden Grows

How do we start our garden?
With clean and fertile soil
Castings of worms, bones of dinosaurs,
Tears of mothers over fallen children,
Tumbled star dust in the crucible of a tree.

How do we plant our seeds?
We tuck them into their warm beds, with serenades and chants and ancient stories
Spilling water, spilling energy injected from our eyes to their leaves
Curious about what will emerge next.

How do we love our garden?
We gently weed, we watch for stress, we teach ourselves to listen for unspoken pleas for help
So flowers and fruits can appear
As the lichen and fungus wait in the distance to claim what nurture neglects.

What will our garden share with us?
The most delicate forget-me-nots, the most gentle daisies and lilies
The most fragrant gardenias, frangipanis, and jasmine
The most brilliant hibiscus and bougainvillea
The most sumptuous rose
The most curious orchid
The brightest sunflower
The tallest poppy
And the most magnificent lotus.

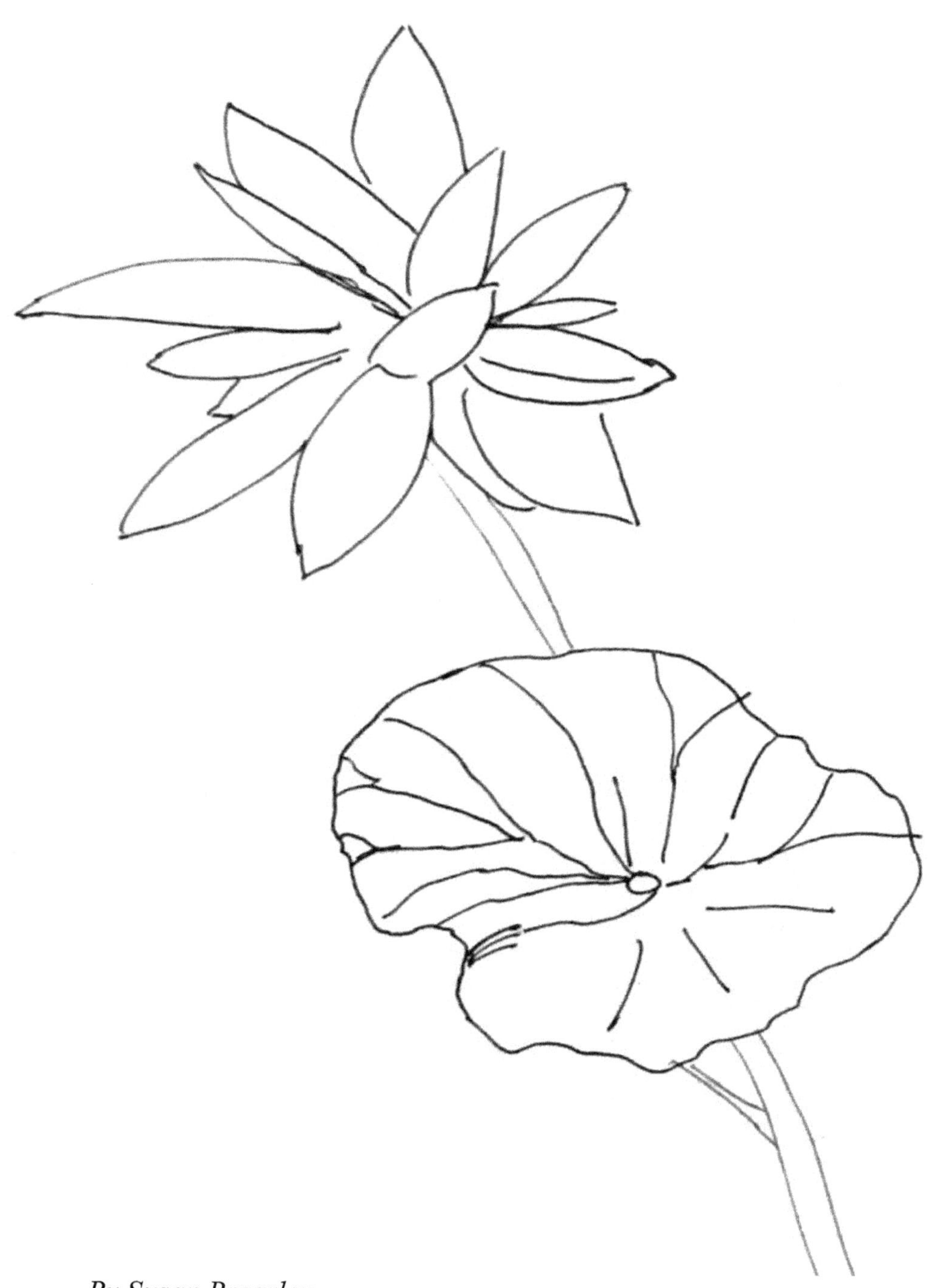

By Susan Brearley

Anu Anniah

Anu Anniah recently discovered her quill and ink pot and is rather unstoppable. She is exploring her views and voice through poetry, humor, and slice-of-life articles. Anu recently published “Eye Am In Denial”, a collection of light-hearted stories.

Instagram: anu_anniah_writes

Where Night Owls Fly Free

She loved the night
the silence, that one chirruping cricket
she wandered about on the streets
the world a labyrinth of silence
her friends, the creatures of the night
the tawny owl, the broody bat
the cat with eyes shining iridescent

She loved the night
the inkiness
Inviting. She could dip a quill and write
the only sound her footsteps on gravel
crunch after delicious crunch

She loved the night
the moon, oh the mesmerizing moon
she was of water
how powerful the pull of the moon
the boys laughing, chattering in the corner
enjoying the night just like her
She loved the night

Gritsy

They hated their uncle
that sweet man
who showered them with love
too much love, touchy feely love
Mom shushed their rants
"He's your uncle," she whispered

Alka began to fight him
clawed at him, screamed, kicked
he laughed
Daya kept calm, way too calm, wooden
Alka was confused
"Does Daya enjoy it?"

At the farm the two teenage girls
draw water at the well
a dark shadow, the uncle
Alka withdraws, he follows
Daya watches, hawk-eyed, biding time
A swift leg shoots out, trips
Uncle in the well
Screaming! Gurgling! Silence
The end of a love they would not miss.

Somewhere in the world

Somewhere in the world
a scene magical, I hear
forever lovely and cool and green
exists a place, a place of dreams

Beauteous and wonderous
rolling green hills
cascading waterfalls
vines and flowers
endless green meadows

Somewhere in the world
peace and tranquility
love and harmony
comfort and care
everything magical
a dreamland, I hear

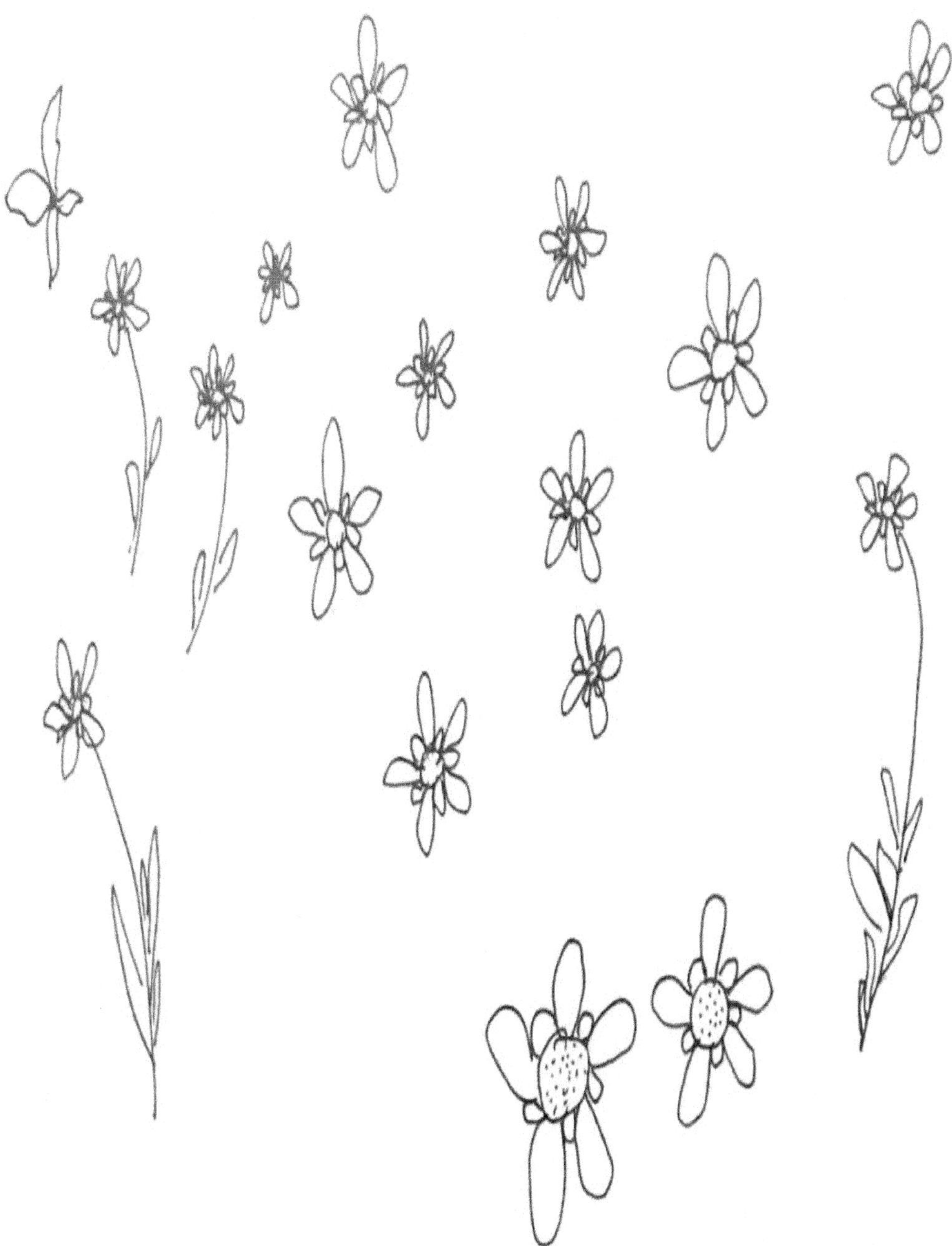

By Susan Brearley

Drishnaa Sharma

I am thirteen, a very new teen and what makes me tick are colours on canvas, feminist art and off-the-beaten-track artists. I follow several on social media. I spend most of my day dreaming, getting inspired, painting (my driving force) and dealing with homework (not passionate about it at all!). Getting published is a daydream I am working towards. Living in this moment and art-ing my way into it.

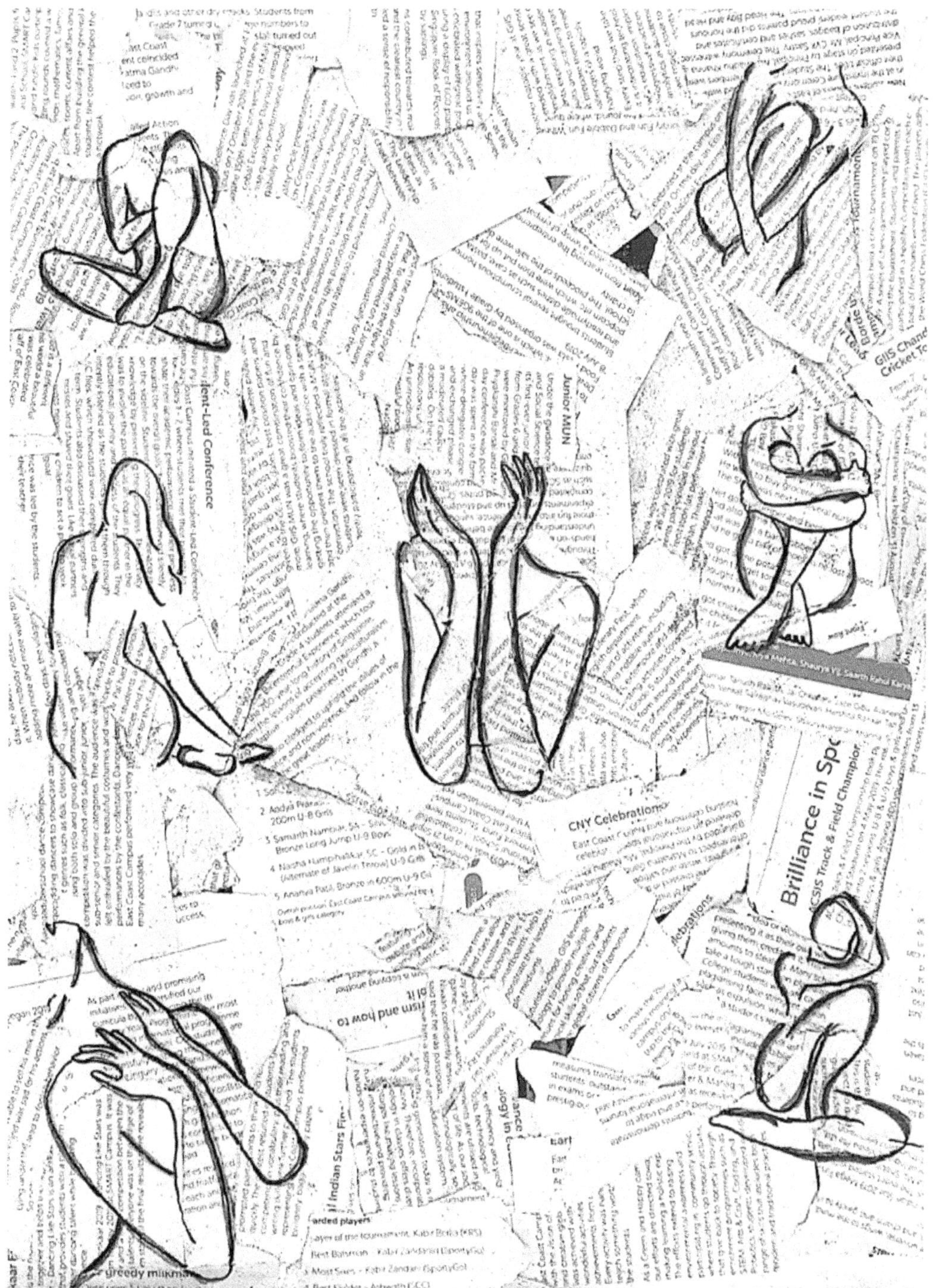

By *Drishnaa Sharma*

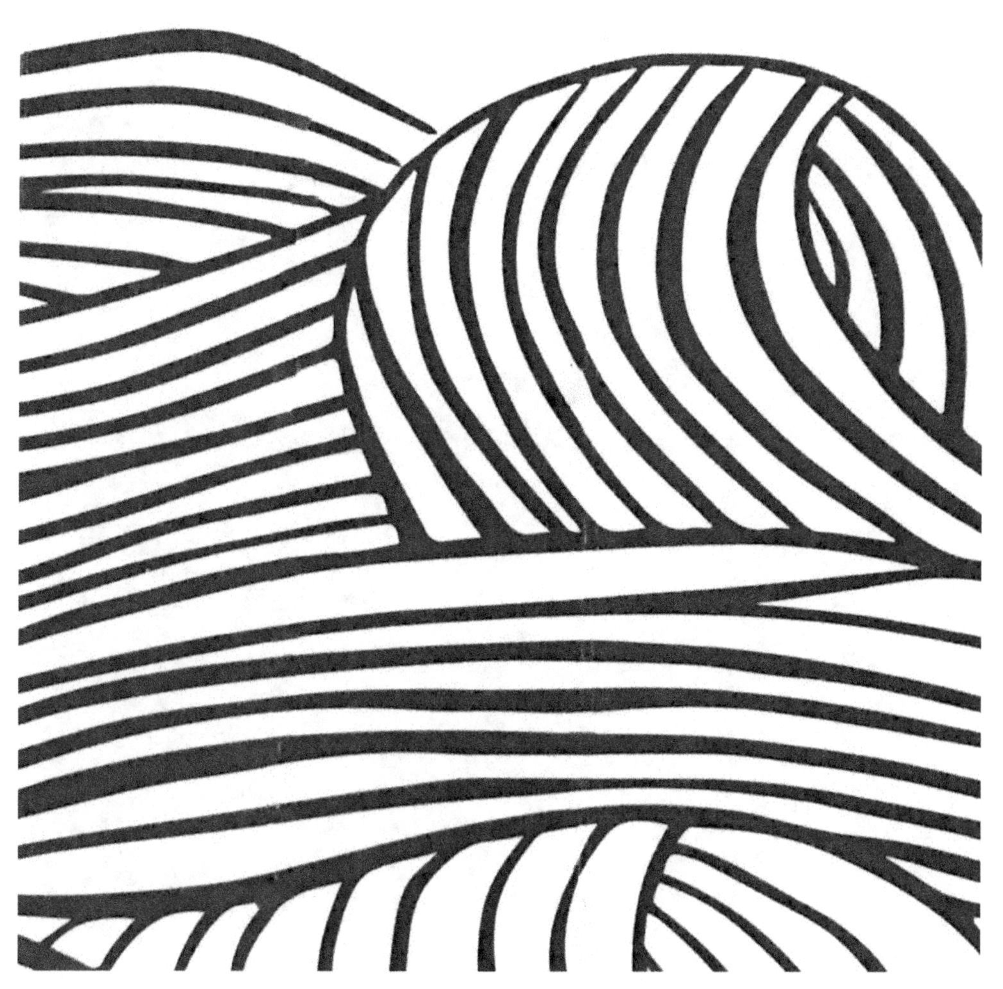

By Susan Brearley

Jennifer Gehl

Jennifer Gehl is the author of The Return of Planet Sedna: Astrology, Healing, and the Awakening of Cosmic Kundalini, and The Science of Planetary Signatures in Medicine: Restoring the Cosmic Foundations of Healing. As a musician, astrologer, and healer, she brings astrological wisdom to life with sound, rhythm, and harmony.

Uranus

Thunderbolts that fill the sky
and trigger shock and awe
Rebels and outsiders who
refuse to bend and bow
Genius minds that innovate
inventing new solutions
And those who revolutionize
to improve the human condition
All of this and more are the instincts I awaken
Storms can be predicted
Not my moment of revelation

Chiron

Bridging you to worlds beyond
I show you how to heal
What you've been may not in fact
be what you wish to feel
Ancient wounds must come to light
for you to mend your soul
Mortal and immortal both
must blend to make you Whole
This is what I offer you
Receive my benediction
for as you heal, others too,
Release their own affliction

Sedna

My higher dimensions call to you
to face your lowest lows
The paradox of going within
transcends the path you chose
Your destiny for the future lies
not in repeating the past
I represent that part of you
that won't abide the typecast
Your ancestors speak to you through me:
"There is magic in your blood"
By healing your ocean of consciousness
you avoid the cataclysmic flood

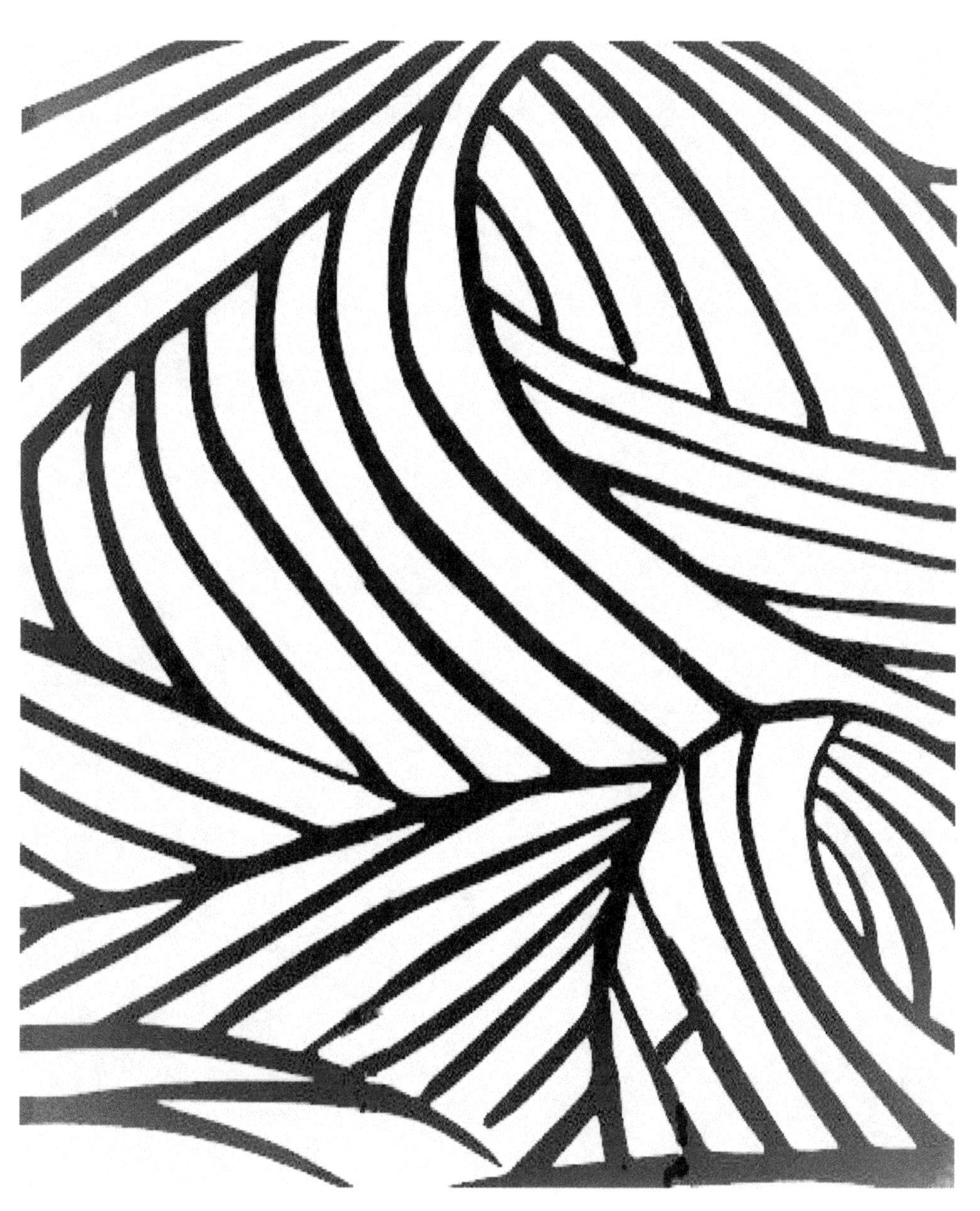

Susan Brearley

Jill Sharon Kimmelman

Jill Sharon Kimmelman, a Pushcart Prize nominee, in poetry.

Recent Publications, Vita Brevis Press, Spillwords Press, Fine Lines, Love of Food, multiple anthologies.

"You Are The Poem", 3-themed debut collection w/original photos, release date, 11-13-2021.

Passions: reading aloud, cooking, photography, theatre.
She lives in Delaware, USA, w/her husband Tim, proud mother of Jordan.

Emerging

This barrel of grief, once hollow, black
without floor or perch, frightens me a little less
with each rung of the climbing out

I am a traveller gazing upon vistas of tranquility
a gift of lanterns light my way, opalescent pearls
and magic beads illuminate the pale dawn

When I stumble on unfamiliar roads, my dress
is rimmed with mystic dust
so I walk a little slower, no need to hurry this journey

Sweet temptation beckons beneath the invitation
of this stranger's welcome smile
I bend like a willow to show a fellow traveler
the grace of my limbs and the recognition in my eyes

This has the makings of healing magic.

You Knew

All my life I limped alone, hid my scars in silent shame,
kept a tight hold on my cane. Now I wear shirts that bare
my arms without a care, my eyes fill up with tears when I
see you standing there. Who knew that my life would no
longer be the same…you knew

Who knew I would ever be loved, find a perfect woman
for my wife. We exchanged rings beneath a prayer shawl
for two. It's perfect, it's right, it's forever.
Who knew I would ever be so happy…you knew

My limp is more pronounced, you need a knee that's new.
Who knew that my memories are of joyful things we
have yet to do, a path blazing toward our eternity.
God blessed me with you…you knew.

Created with Tim Little

Joyce Rufus

I am Joyce Rufus; I have been a High School teacher for over 3 decades. Though I have worn different hats during this journey, I feel at best when I'm in the classroom. I believe the role of a teacher is not to teach but rather to awaken the creative knowledge in each child.

Slow Down
(Dedicated to 2020 and 2021)

Life had to lock down,
Humanity, slow down
To recharge and regrow
To replenish melted snow,
To rethink relationships
To restore friendships,
To rest and stop racing
To lend and stop taking,
To heal and not hurt
To give, not subvert,
To love and not lust
To embrace, not distrust
To stop and to stare
To feel and to share,
To subdue our big ego
To forgive and to let go,
To dream and watch sunset
To allow nature some rest,
To count our many blessings
To ensure we've learnt lessons.
To appreciate not strife
This wild and precious life

Serenity

I look for you in all I do,
In sunset and the morning dew
In gentle murmur of the breeze
In swaying passion of the trees

I look for you in all I see,
In rolling waves full of glee
In sweet fragrance of a flower
In every moment of every hour

I look for you to cheer me on
When I am down and forlorn
I look in gentle sounds and sights
All around me, days and nights.

And when I find thee I know how
Amidst chaos, the flowering bough
Bends low to touch the sparkling stream
Quiet, calm, unfazed, like a dream.

A new Dawn

His deafening silence
His unreachable heart
His cold indifference
His callous disregard
Were all so real.

Her warm sincere feelings
Her fervent desires
Her sentimental cries
Her heart full of fire
Were also real

This human encounter
She should've known
To obey and be silent
Not try and move stone

Her crystal dream shattered
imagined in youth
As shards lay scattered
Reflecting the truth

She picked up her cases
Though confidence was low
looked straight at her nemesis
Walked out of the door

Fate held her hand tightly
Destiny too took care
On Pegasus she soared
her spirit repaired.

Katalina Gutierrez

Katalina's art practice is a process of poetics, meditation, and transfiguration. She creates fiction shorts, works in documentary projects, and teaches art to the youth. Her dream is to write and illustrate a children's picture book. Currently, she resides in New York. You can find her at KatalinaStudio.com

Black Coral

As I glance back, my body, now feather like—
awakens from a chamber of coral.

Astral beings sail through aquatic
plants in a whimsical light.

Shaped by many names that blaze into
one another… infinitely.

Fluorescence dressed as dragons—their
glimmering skin precedes human history.

They enter and leave the room
with no one noticing.

Their silhouettes appear to be still—
moving through water like shadows.

Walking back on the bridge, the black
elliptical eyes find mine.

Kathy Jo Bryant

Kathy Jo Bryant hails from California, USA. She is an author and has received many certificates and awards for her poetry. Her work is in a growing number of published anthologies. She is a member of, and former moderator for, the growing Facebook poetry group: The Passion of Poetry

The Rigors of Life

We push against the rigors of life
Stand up to its challenges strong
We don't fold, when things don't fly

Sometimes we feel we can't endure
Struggles melt away all our sap
Then we get a burst of determination

We look to our future & get a second wind
This core feeling to be brave, helps us win
It is our survival space, a God-given gift!

That Place, That Space

So, have you found it yet
Without getting upset

That place that is a space
So bravery you'll embrace?

Don't cower in dread fear
Take courage, get in gear!

The world must have the brave
And through their love to save

Those hopeless helpless souls
Those wrecked upon life's shoals

Stand up, be counted, then
So, you'll have a great win-win!

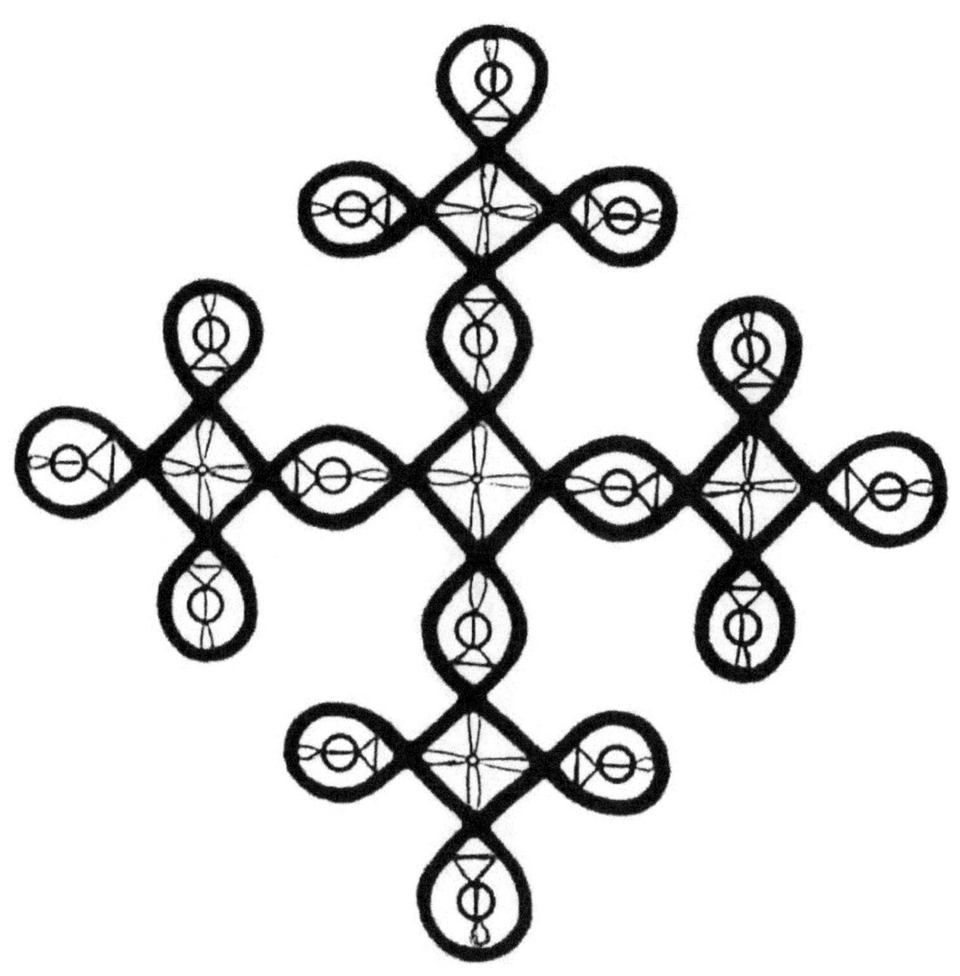

By Kathy Jo Bryant

Lauren Salkin

Dysfunctional wife, mother, loser of stuff, Lauren spends her days making sense out of the chaos that spins in her ADHD head.

Writer of humor, satire, poetry, and thought pieces, Lauren's work has appeared on *Huffington Post, Extra Newsfeed, Literally Literary, MuddyUm, The Haven, ByLine,* and *Shroud Magazine.*

Village of Light

welcomes me home
in a blanket of words
soothing
renewing
hugging my heart
in an embrace
of shared values
inspiring
mindfulness
a promise of give-and-take
in a mystical place
where gardens grow from the touch
of nourishing souls
hope
burgeoning
vibrant
welcoming
a beacon
calling me home

Lisa Bolin

A published writer and poet, Lisa creates from her archipelago home in the Baltic Sea. Originating from Australia, the natural world inspires her. Lisa is an avid reader, sharing her love of language and life through teaching, creating, writing, and discussing with people from all over the world.
Instagram: lisabolinwrites

She is Me

She wrapped sea and forest
around her shoulders.
A cloak of moss, seagrass, salt,
pine needles, stone, and birch.
Soothing her skin, nourishing her heart,
filling her lungs with hope-tinged sweetness.
She embraced an archipelago.
Shimmering islands in a glistening sea.
She took them into her being,
cherishing each twig, pebble, seed.
Rolling new words on her tongue,
singing new songs, making new meaning.
The leap she took, a free-fall,
landed her in a space, a place,
with grace. Courage.
She pulled the cloak, tight,
safe in the knowledge,
this was her place.

In Your Own Skin

loving, whole, light,
an open mind and heart
blooming, fresh, bright
now is the time to start

protected, snug, secure,
breathing in, breathing out
luminous, vibrant, sure
free of any doubt

soft, warm, glowing,
sitting peacefully, within
sparkling, twinkling, growing
safe in your own skin

The Space

Is it far up high in the clouds above?
Between the twinkling stars
and the pale, full moon?
Is it curled in a boat
set afloat on watery waves?
Wrapped in a rug and the arms
of the one you love most?
Is it floating, water caressing my back?
As I look to the heavens,
space and beyond, dreaming,
Sounds muffled by my watery cocoon.
Is it inside myself? Deep down?
Heart beating blood
Red, breathing fire, careful
Eyes aglow as I reach down
Out, to the universe, and within.
For the space. Safe. Brave.

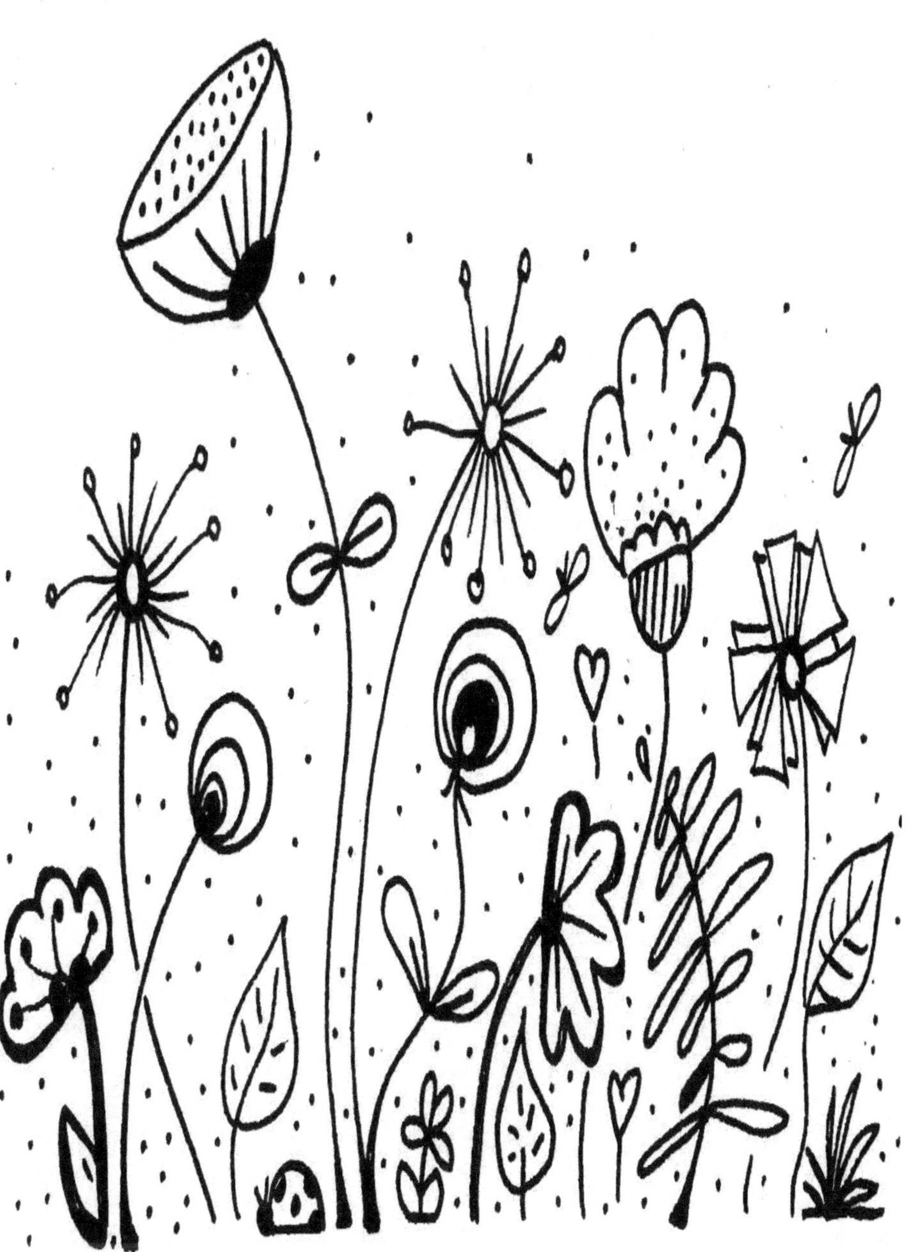

By Lisa Bolin

Lisa Tomey

Lisa Tomey is a poet, writer, and artist from Raleigh, NC. Publications include Heart Sounds chapbook, Heart Beats-editor and contributing author, Silver Linings, anthologies, and several literary publications. She edits for Fine Lines Literary Journal. She is an ambassador for Garden of Neuro. As manager of Prolific Pulse Press LLC, she promotes quality poetry.

she loved the night

the silence—

the only sound her footsteps on gravel

crunch after delicious crunch

yet—that one annoying cricket

the creatures of the night

the tawny owl, the broody bats

the cat with eyes shining iridescent

she loved the night

the inkiness

she could dip a quill and write

she loved the night

the moon, oh the mesmerizing moon

she was of water

which explains the tug

the exasperation when a cloud passed

the boys laughing, chattering in the corner

enjoying the night just like her

yes, she loved the night

When I Dream – A Haibun

When I dream, I go places where my body can't go, an escape of sorts. You see, I have just enough body left to get me to a long age. There is just a short circuit to my bones and oh the muscles, they get grumpy too. But my mind, it can go places and when I dream, I get to travel the best places ever. Did you know I have traveled the world in my dreams. I felt no discomfort. I may have flung about, willy nilly, to the whims of wonder. In my dreams, I have pillows for my feet. I walk on water. I fly. I feel nothing and yet everything that comes from the freedom. Yet, I am not ready to leave this life to pursue those dreams, but to let bravery take a stab at the more for me in this planet earth, as long as she will have me and when she won't I will go out into the sea and commence my dreams. My safe space is my dreams, and my brave space is my life. I wouldn't have it any other way.

When I dream, I'm free

Life gives me chances to sleep

Living gives choices

A Gentle Breeze

whispers to my mind
how to remember when once
was not enough for me
love would be another surrender
living in another's dreams
when I had to realize
my unicorn comes but once
and with this I ride away
I learnt that I must be brave
in order to truly know life

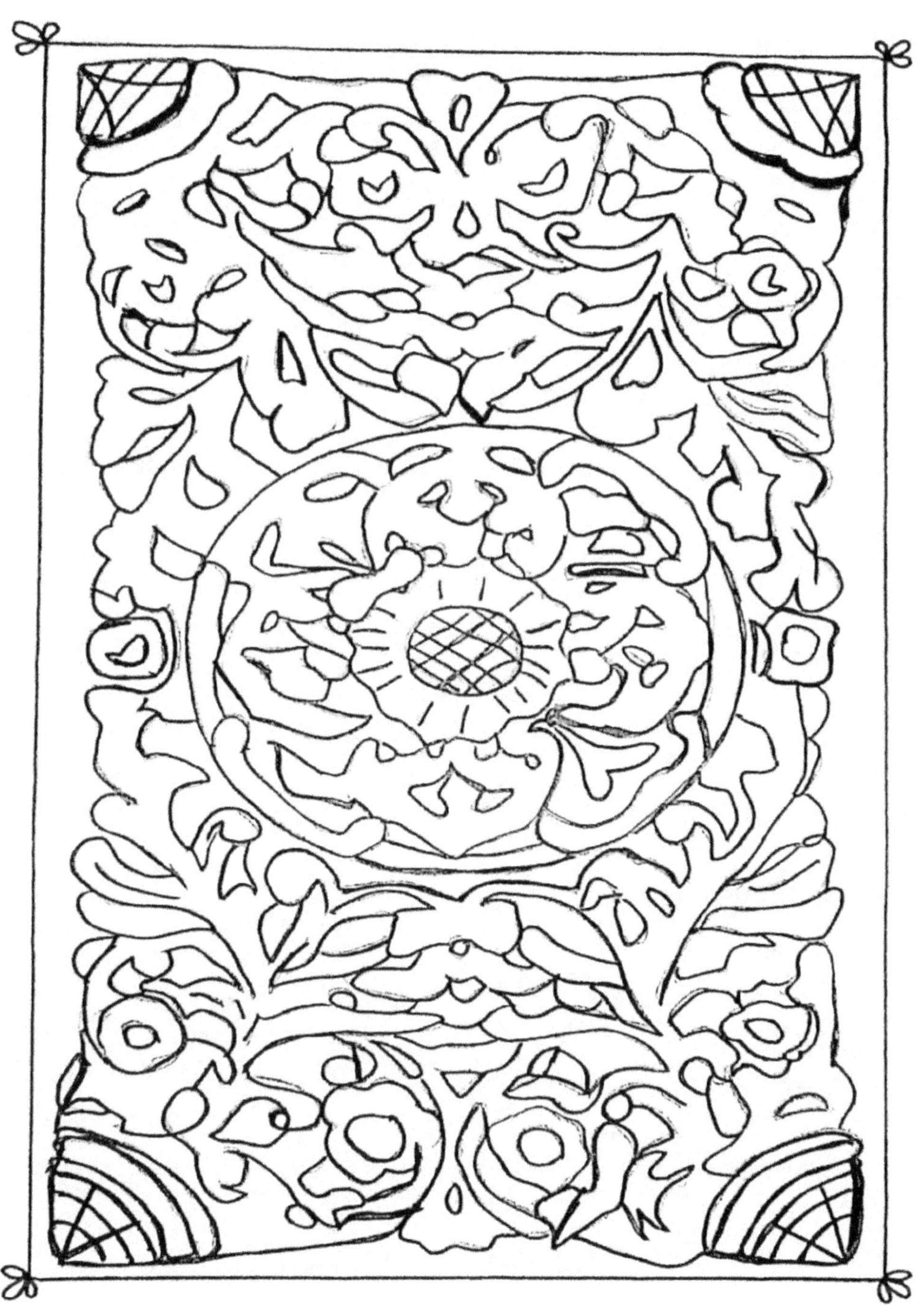

By Lisa Tomey

Maria Editha Garma-Respicio

Country: Philippines
Workplace: Hong Kong

She holds a Diploma in Nursing, Physical Therapy, Computer Science, English Literature. She started writing short stories, poems, and prose during her primary years. She participated in different anthologies worldwide. She's a member of various international poetry groups and has won several awards. Currently, she's working in Hong Kong.

Xenial Relationship

She's the vagabond, wearing clothes unkempt
Trying every initiative to preempt
Any situations that may cause disturbance
So police will not shoo away her existence.

Couldn't measure how deep's her torment
Only this i know, big's her predicament
She might be a victim of life's infliction
Never got the chance to retaliate or bounce.

Woe to her, any attempt
To halt her sufferings in vain, she's inept
How could i dry the tears of despondence?
She's definitely not society's abhorrence.

Giving alms not enough, she must be adept
In dealing and fighting every tempts
Be xenial to the bum, show care not ignorance
Lucky you never walked her shoes, so give reverence.

My Knight

I have faith that in all circumstance,
We can withstand the storm and prevail.
No hurdles can block the burning romance,
My ethereal consort in the trail.
In the gloom, you ignite the torch of hope.
You complement my life like no other.
In adversities, we'll triumph and cope.
Indeed, you made me stronger and tougher.
Darling, hold my hand tight, do not let it go.
Let's make our dreams into reality.
Bright stars witness our undying vow,
And bless our union till eternity.
I'm confident, i'll wear the victor's hat,
For you keep the lamp burning just like that.

It Takes Tenacity To Succeed

In order to reach the peak of the mountain
We need to have a positive disposition
That every difficulty, we'll conquer it up
Fear should be eradicated, and so the word quit.

We need to have a great vision of what will be accomplished
And enthusiasm to achieve the goals established
Mind power over any physical pain
Whining be avoided, so we can pass the terrain.

An adventurous spirit, a risk taker
Never an easy feat, it's an assiduous labour
That's why we need to have endurance
And be thine friend to perseverance.

But the crown's awaits at the top
The pristine scenic view's waving at the summit
The golden sun's towering the magical sights
The determined soul will reap the hard work price.

Michelle Chermaine Ramos

Michelle Chermaine Ramos is a self-taught multidisciplinary artist, inspirational storyteller, writer, and journalist in Toronto, Canada. Raised in the U.A.E and being of Filipino, Spanish, and Japanese descent, she wields the power of art to connect the threads of different cultures to find magic in everyday life.
Instagram: michellechermaine

Don't Forget Yourself

A comforting touch, a listening ear,
A cheerful word to clear sad tears,
Kind eyes that see and understand,
The priceless gift of a helping hand,
Ever so present to hold near and dear
Together through weather both stormy and clear.

In being their haven, you must recall
You cannot always do it all.
Don't let your energy and time dry up.
You cannot pour from an empty cup.
To your own needs you too must attend
The way you would a cherished friend.
This crucial lesson you must learn:
You deserve the same love you give in return.

Nanci Arvizu

Creative Creator Nanci Arvizu has stepped into the life she designed by writing down her words and giving them up to the universe to manifest into reality.

Garden Words

Sanctuary
Abundance
Fate
Experience
Attraction
Neuroscience
Dream
Believe
Receive
Attract
Visualize
Enlightenment
Synchronicity
Peace
Awareness
Create
Expansion

Dark Light

1,483,722 words and a tube of chapstick
the words added up, the balm rolls in the drawer
reminders not to forget
a bond built on respect and a shared love of stories
stolen in the night by an intrusive kiss of death
the future now uncertain
fear became anger and swallowed an existence.

Somewhere in the darkness
an unknown seed sprouted
reaching for light it
knew without knowing existed.

Slowly growing until all of a sudden
it was bigger than even the seed
believed it could become
the path leading
out of the soil
and into the sun.

Untitled

And a leaf turned over revealing her true self to herself. While some of the world was shocked, and some of it was awed, a perfect portion of the people could see her truth, and knew she was one of them.

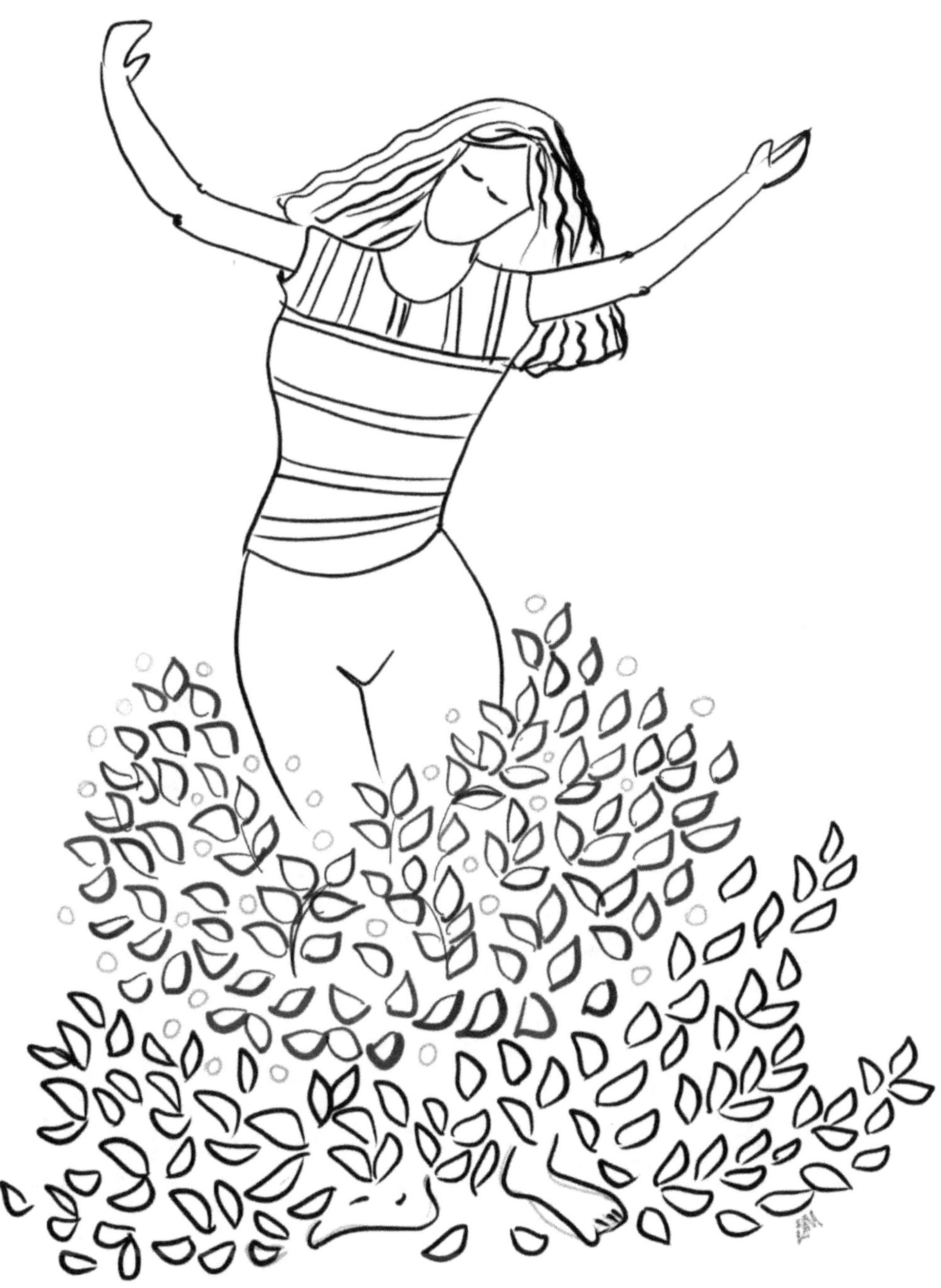

By Seemra Misra

Pratibha Savani

Pratibha Savani is a poet and artist from the UK. Her debut book, Tangles + Knots, uniquely combines her art and writing with mindfulness and wellbeing themes. Inspired by nature, science and spirituality, creativity is a key element in her explorative writing, cultivating her artistic style, including her bite-sized mindfulness quotes on Instagram and Facebook - Pratibha Poetry Art.

In This Space

Space
The only place
Far enough away
In my conscious brain
To release my thoughts
Drop it in, my virtual inbox
And file it away
Free my mind
In this space
Let my creative side begin
Away from daily distractions
A brilliant way to know
I can stay
In this space
Bring alignment within
Lock unwanted garbage, away
Switch off
In this space
Peace and order, rejuvenates
I can see clearly
In this space
Where I want to be
And know I have it
EVERYDAY

Snuggly Wrapped

Snuggly wrapped
In the wilderness of trees
In my winter coat
Hat and gloves
The open cold air
Revives my thoughts
Wind whizzes by
And moves me a little closer
To that open space
With all the lined up trees
Its beautiful gardens
With the geometric patched flowerbeds
An outline
Of where they used to be
To decorate the green
That I am sitting in the middle of
And bravely facing my inner emotions
In the cold winter sun
Hugging myself
As a realisation has begun
If flowers can flourish back
Then...
In this open space
I know I CAN

mysterious magic

you are my **lantern**

shining bright

each time I look **up**

waiting for your **light**

your **mysterious** magic

makes me feel **divine**

as I look on **up**

to **search** for you

each **night**

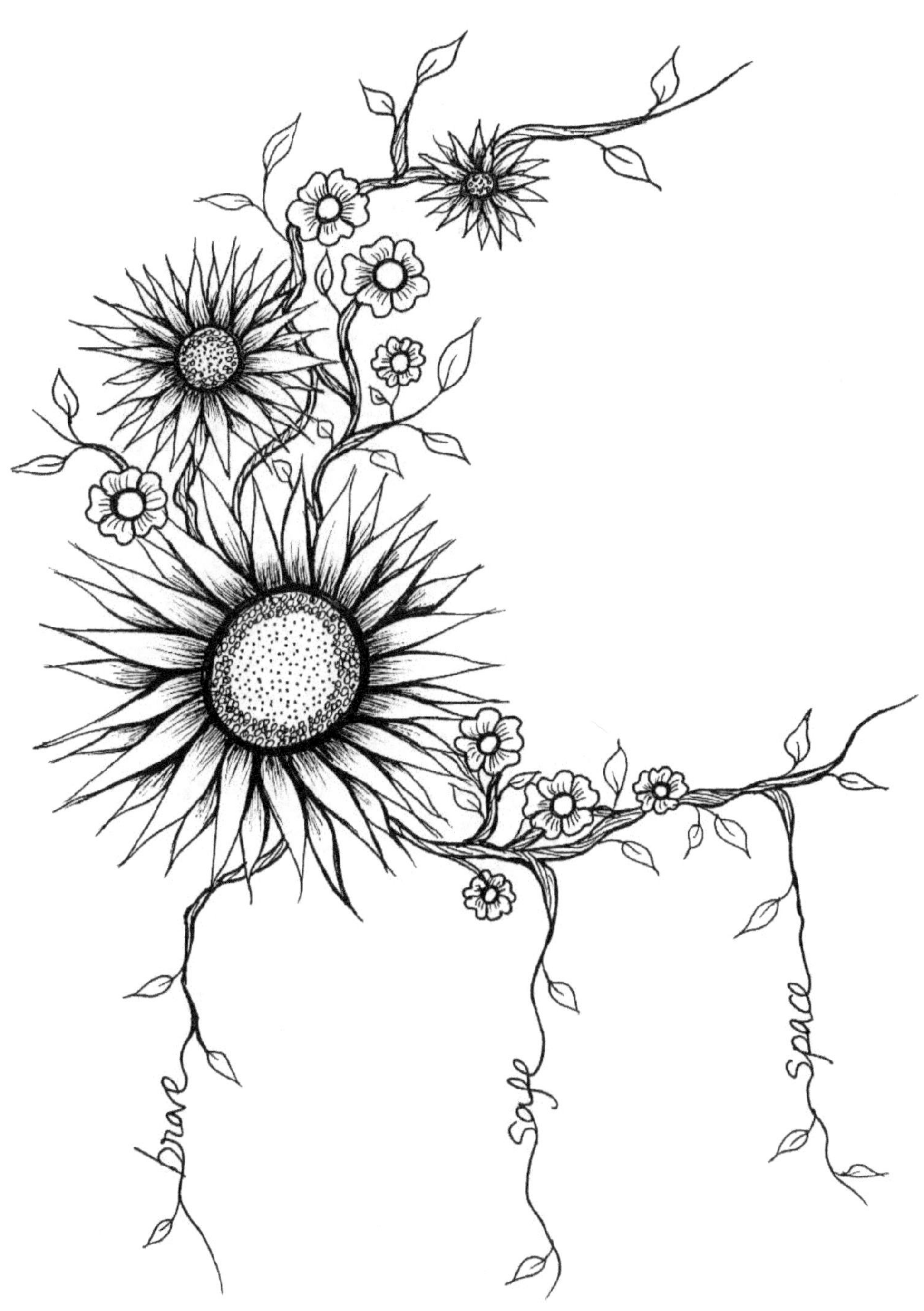

By Pratibha Savani

Preeti Mistry

Preeti Mistry is an Artist and Designer from the UK, she is inspired by drawing patterns, mandalas, black and white art and painting art with dots. She has interests in Jewellery Making, Paper Quilling Art, Mix Media and is specialized in Floral Designs.

Instagram: preeti_little_things and Preetiflowers

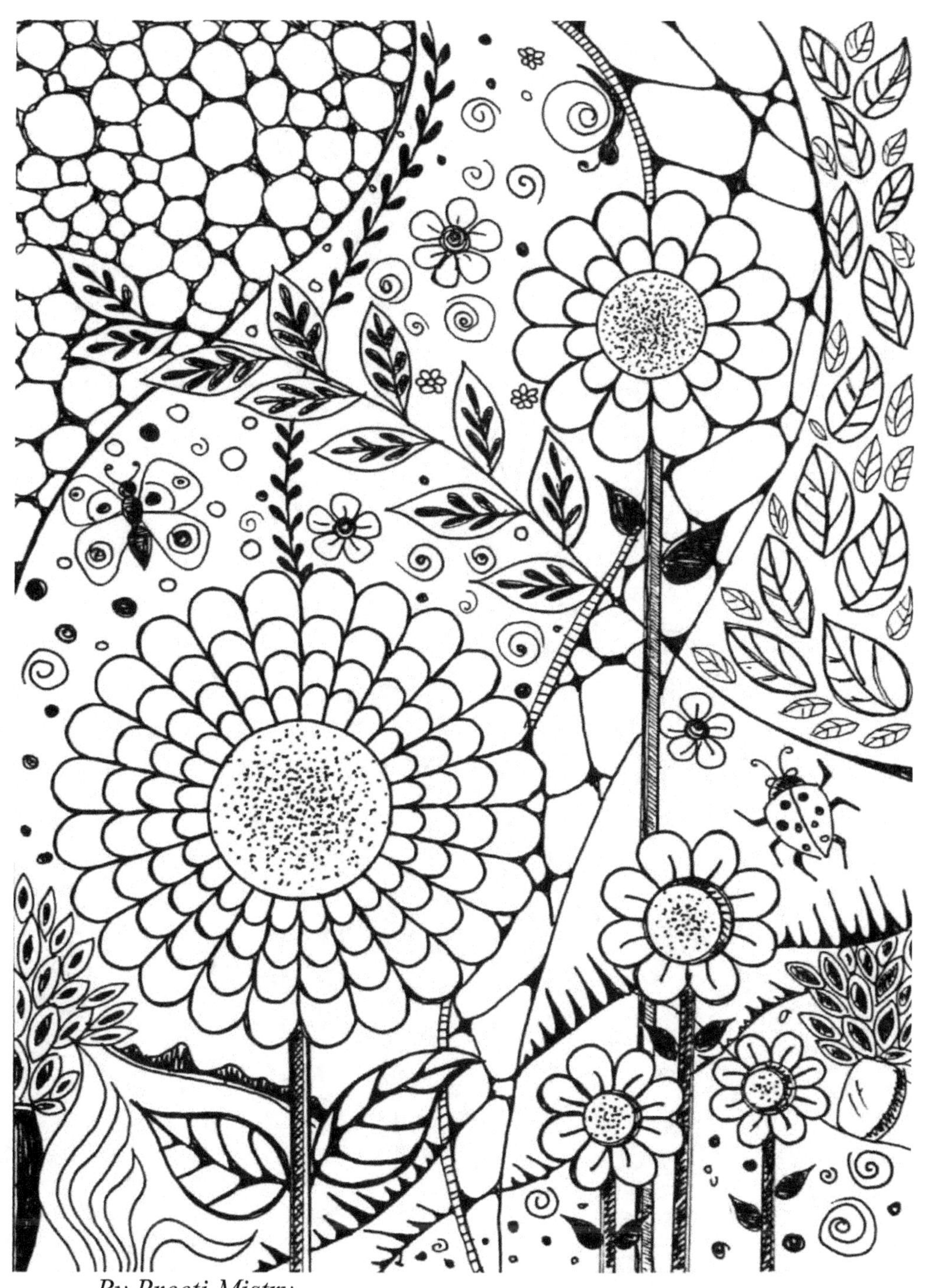

By Preeti Mistry

Priya Ranganathan

Priya Ranganathan is from Bangalore, India and has been a programmer, project manager, soft-skills trainer, and interior designer. She has written manuals for software, medical, human resources, training workshops and even for art portfolios. She dabbles in music, writing, sewing, and enjoys time with her son Rayan.

About Us

I don't know how to describe 27 years, and jot it down in a few lines
I don't know how to portray a friendship, which brighter than the sun shines.

You sat in front at school, a teacher's pet, hands raised
While a back-bencher was I, avoiding the questions which left me dazed.
Yet somehow a camaraderie built, in the early hours before class
Laughter shared; boys discussed; not one topic allowed to pass.

You travelled 8000 miles for my wedding, forsaking a job and a dream
And stood behind me all throughout, so that I didn't come apart at the seam.

There are so many incidents I cannot forget; the thief who stole your bike
The man who owned an MF Hussain; that silly professor you didn't like.
That creepy train station at night; the first jeans I forced you to buy;
That luscious wobbly chocolate cake; or the time when you-know-who got high!

We have gone through every tough time, battled each other's critics
Been there for beginnings and partings, through all the lifts and kicks.

My son knows who is on the phone, as my voice drops to a whisper

Giggling, gossiping, grumbling. Is that Aunty? You laugh the most with her!
There are so many stories yet to be told; countless journeys we will still face
I can’t describe what you mean to me. You are my safest and bravest place.

Untitled

Online school has started. Little fingers tap over the keyboard.
High-pitched good mornings pipe in. Reedy voices sing the school prayer.
Some confident, some fumbling.

The day unfolds into a colourful imaginary world
Filled with animals, and snow-clad mountains
Multiplication sums, and patriotic songs
Moralistic stories, and scientific paper boats.
The ideas trip over, stumbling.
Messy paintbrushes, and online codes
Quizzes, games, mind-maps, dictation
Sigh, and some messaging, gaming on the sly.
Jumbling, tumbling.

The pretty girl sings a song, fervently cheered on by her fans.
The grinning boy plays his latest piano tune. Bro, that's just awesome!
The gruff-voiced kid shows his painting. Brushstrokes beyond his years.
Clapping hands, oohs and aahs. No question of grumbling.

Dreams of unfinished submissions, of incomplete activities, of non-existent projects.
And the only reward is the smile that breaks out from the quietest.
The answer which tumbles out of the unsure-est.
The patient pause given by the loudest. And the question asked by the shyest.
Dedicated to all the teachers who make school safe and brave.
Truly humbling.

Home

A room

To sleep in and call my own.

A mother

Whose caress gives comfort like no other.

A son

Grubby little fingers that clutch my heart tight.

A sister

To share all the sunsets with.

A husband

Who turns to me for strength.

A niece

With a heart of gold.

Friends

With whom I can just be free.

Cousins

Who have shared my life.

An enchanting book waiting to be read;

A haunting song to sing out loud.

A warm balcony overlooking the beach;

Lilting rain among the dark trees.

All places

Which the mind calls home.

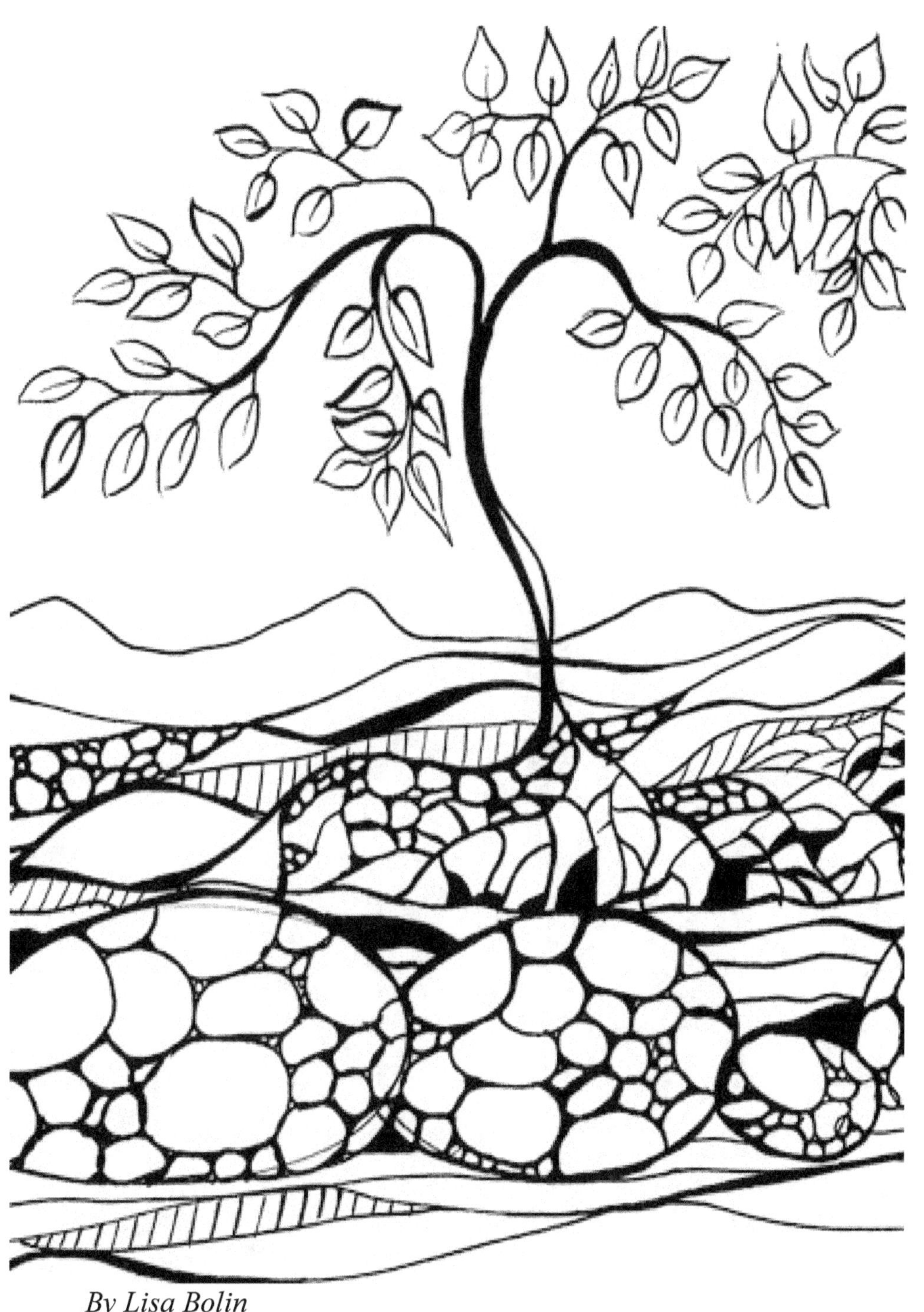

By Lisa Bolin

Priyanka Chowdhury

Priyanka Chowdhury is a dentist based in Melbourne, Australia. She hails from a family with a strong medical background. An avid academician with a strong aesthetic bent of mind, her work reflects the synchronisation of art and poetry. She strives to share her life experiences to inspire others.

A Garden Like Mine

Eden was just a name
And no garden has ever been the same:
In plenty and abundance thrived
Where man was unstained and kind.
No hunger, no conflict or crime
Survived in a garden of the kind.
Every garden is cultured
Bearing the burden of time:
Seeds and weed compete,
Flowers bloom finding some room;
The golden blade sways-
Some sun, some rain
Nature's inherence has always reigned.
A gardener of an innate kind
Adapts to a different green,
Glides like the pollen unseen;
When flowers in surprise bloom
The thoughts would've made enough room;
Where such a mind finds a home,
A safe and brave garden grows.

Reena Bhatnagar

I grew up in the North Indian city of Lucknow, known for its culture and food. Being a Loreto girl is a significant highlight of my life, a school that encouraged me to be myself. I have a deep passion for reading, which is a great source of joy to me. I completed a Masters in Literature which further deepened my passion for reading and writing. I moved to Australia in 2003 and I am a Teacher by profession. My other passions are Music and Travel.

Love

There is this feeling that lies within
And grows as time goes by
An all-encompassing sentiment
That's there for kith and kin

It stretches and ne'er contracts
Like an unceasing ocean
A boundless affection
How truly beautiful and abstract!

Our World

"Imagine there's no heaven…"
The famous words of the song fill the air
Urging us to think yet again
Can our world unite
To create a Safe and Brave Space?

A world free of
Greed and avarice
Covetousness and Jealousy
Selfish endeavour
And Discrimination

Let us unite to design
A Safe and Brave Space
For our young'uns to thrive

Reena Nag

Raleigh, NC & North Caldwell, NJ

An aspiring writer, Reena has spent 20 years on Wall Street at Barclays, Lehman Brothers and Morgan Stanley in research, operations and technology. While her work (for pay) nurtured her left brain, her work (for love of home & community) delighted her right brain. At the end of the day both left her happily exhausted.

Reena has dabbled in Pandemic poetry & prose that she summoned the courage to publish on LinkedIn.

LinkedIn: Reena-Nag

A Safe and Brave Space

We are forty-nine point six per cent
Women
They are fifty-one point four
Let's create a safe brave space
To a safe, brave world ensured.
One hundred per cent in this together

Together, we must strive
to create a space so special
free from all this pain and strife.

Money, fame, fortune buys
many things we often crave
Friendship, laughter, love and like
creates a space that's safe.

After all the people in our world
just like them, you and me
need a safe brave space
a space of liberty.

So, ladies
let's take control
This is our moment
This is why we prod, nudge,
walk the walk and talk the talk.

Because we are Half the Sky.

Untitled

On my bicycle barely a teen
I pedaled fast I didn't want to be seen
7 pm the sun dipping low
faster, faster i must go
through darkening gullies and narrow lanes
vaulting over potholes and open drains

What was i doing out so late?
Was I being brave in tempting fate?
It's never safe for a girl on a bike
to be out riding alone in the dark at night
What was i thinking? Was i thinking at all?
This didn't feel safe nor brave at all

Breathless, exhausted, i finally saw the light
of my safe and brave space i knew i'd be alright
Decades later, that ride in the night
has given me a very clear line of sight
i say to you little girls - do what you might
but learn to pedal fast as you reach for those heights

Untitled

I have a safe and brave space
and it's inside my head
it’s sometimes bruised and battered still
it gets me up and away from dread
away from all that isn’t fun ‘coz i can just
think those awful thoughts away
i love my head for my mind it keeps
unhappiness at bay
no matter what the day or night
what’s whirling there and everywhere
i get inside my head, tuck-in and whisper gently
it’ll all be alright

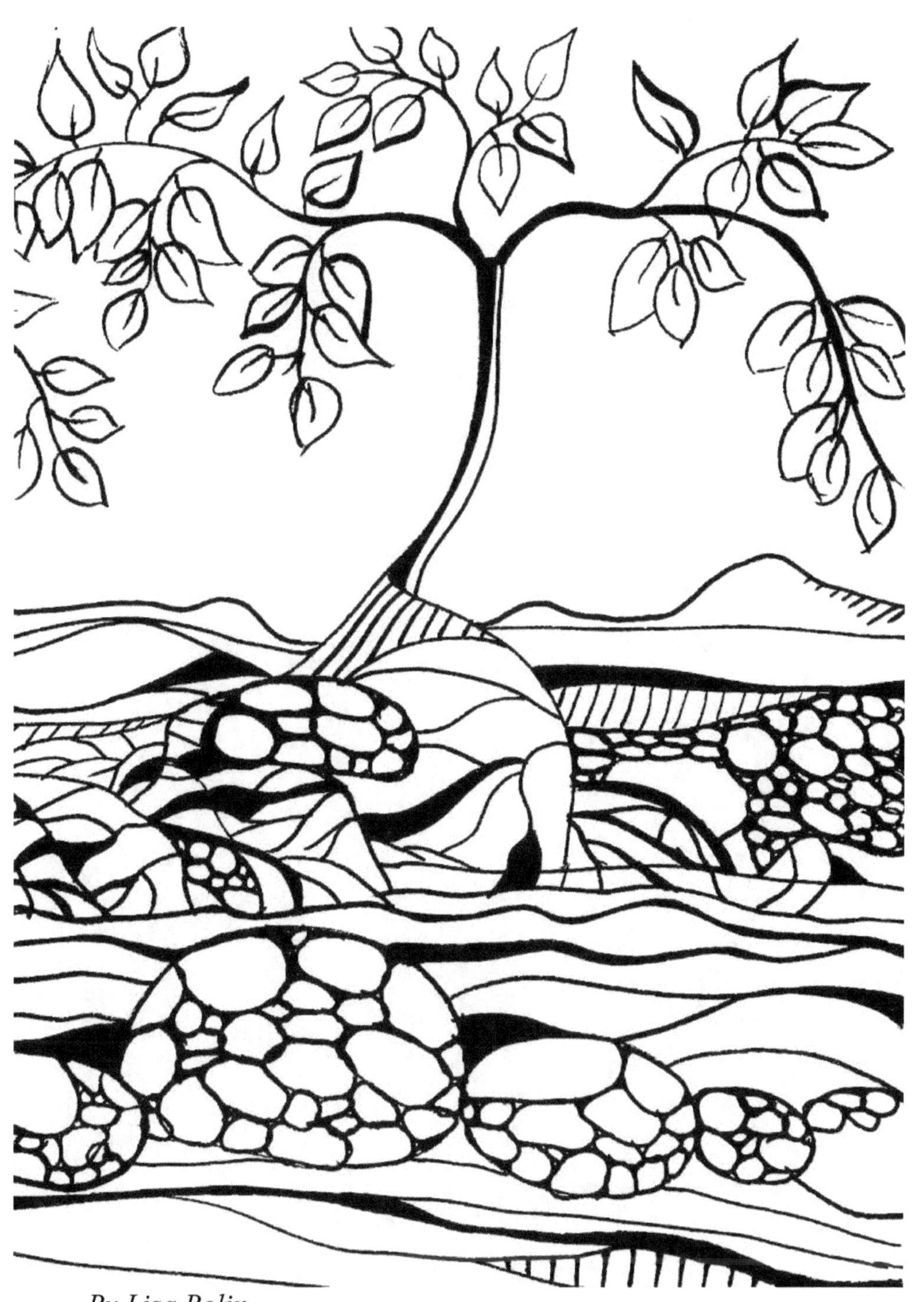

By Lisa Bolin

Richa Sharma

Richa Sharma is a poet, writer, mother of three, 'quadragenarian' who finds adulting a tough business. When not resolving domestic crises wrought by her brood, she's busy eating books and feasting on poetry across the internet. A closet-poet because most of her work for the past three decades has largely been unshared, recent discovery of global poetic communities has enabled her 'coming out' and acceptance publication with a few reputed journals.

Instagram: dryink_brush

Summer Days

Flying scarves have ditched the necks
Harder to find shade along the pool decks
Thighs of tan and honest sunburn
Hazy, refractive desires to turn
Bosoms of afternoons, round, voluptuous
Pale pink smallness of the summer morns
The wistful delicacy of wasted heat
Skirting along the sunlight, deadbeat
Follow in footsteps of the dry, hot run
the burnt crisp leaves offered to the Sun
thirsty hiccups that follow every part
eating and finishing, long days to start
coloured vulgarity of lilies and petulant petunias
sunkissed sunflowers and pansies and plumerias
bent boughs, a pitstop for the brain-parched fickles
sparrows and lost cats, chipmunks and squirrels
day-weary the scorch it drags its feet
spent, waterless, empty, cooked sous-vide
the days then sleep with an orange tan
hurting still and sighing warm
night breeze to foment with a fluffy balm
Summer days are such an unloving muse
A passing hermit, a heartless recluse

Birthing grounds

The earth is still in its labour to birth
No moans, no cries, no pleas to hold hands
It bleeds in its streams and rivers and springs
No shame in its obvious femininity
Brazen sight - its many tall, high breasts
Proud of their nursing, watery veins
Meadows and dunes, forests wild
Dress it, *ensemble,* in its many forms
Worshipped by some, some pagans they are called
No man could be, but woman it bred
right in its image spitting for all to see
like its unstoppable, unabashed fertility
where is that pride buried in civilisational quicksand?
for culture, scripture and 'honour' of man
birthing ground for rape and violation
in her dying dignity, she manages to yell
the volcanoes of her voice vibrate,
erupting forth the magma of molten angst
to bury the filthy animosity,
to burn the prickly foliage of inflicted pain
to renew your bosom with blades of sprouting will
to carve out the rocky roads
to walk without shame, with her ownership of self

Who slapped my butt

Walking down the alleyway, the subway, the back lanes, the bus
I pull down at the hem of my blouse,
covering the object of your limitless lust
I am also pulling up at the same time
From your line of sight, my *décolletage* line
I manage all my many hands
to conceal myself, to make myself safe, to diminish my space
from the front, my breasts, from behind, my butt
from provoking your dirty ire, from falling into my own disgrace
yet I can feel your disrobing me
in full view of the public, in your mind's eye
I am naked, powerless, with no agency
to disown this violation, to gouge out your sight
I am not me, just a fly on the wall
Watching you watch me, watching me squirm
You don't bat an eyelid, no consciousness at all
As you heap upon me the burden of my sex
the burden of fear, all because you think I am less
I cannot beat you if you decided to be a brute
But I will put up a fight, I will raise my voice
I will not walk on silently, mulling in disgust
who among the horde of you, dared to slap my butt

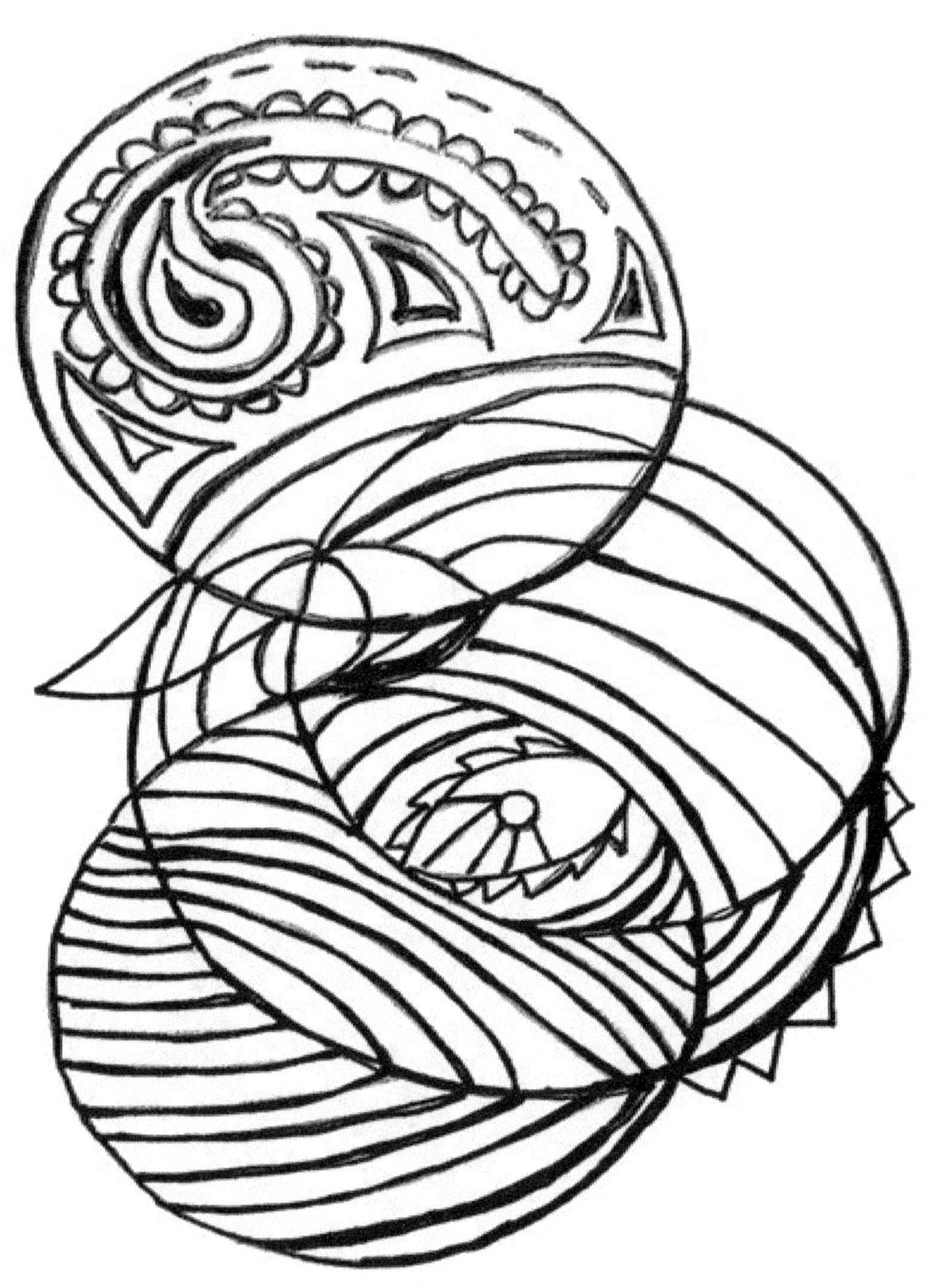

By Lisa Tomey

Robin Klammer

Robin Klammer, age 46, writer and mom, currently lives in a tiny town in Northern Ontario, Canada. She hopes to find her sunny disposition in warmer regions soon. She has a book of poetry and essays called *Words to Light My Way Home*, depicting her struggles through anxiety and depression.

Fly Away From Me

When my thoughts are over run,

It's my brain that wishes to be stunned.

If only for a few brief moments;

So I can breathe deep and exhale all the pollution that clouds my logic.

While carrying out mundane tasks;

I often wonder. "Is this it?!"

Just doing the same thing, day in and day out?

I often want to run

to my room and pout.

But sometimes I shout.

Surely, my purpose is more than what my life has become!

Though most days are plain humdrum.

So it is to daydreams I escape.

Playing word games with no shame.

My own little world without blame.

It's the birds I watch with envy,

Wishing I could fly away and be free!

Sandhya Ranganathan

Sandhya is a dreamer, a Mom, and a globetrotter. She enjoys pottering around her home in Bangalore, India, with her human and feline babies. She has authored *Mia finds a home* and *Burma to Bangalore*, and has contributed poems to anthologies. She expresses her deepest emotions through poetry. Website: *Varnika.co*

Kabuliwali (meaning "Woman from Kabul" in Hindi)

She stares in frustration
at the wall of men
White-robed, with guns
blocking her path.
With tears in her eyes
she clutches her baby to her chest
Turns, and runs down the street
only to find the barrels of a tank
pointed directly at her
the smell of gunpowder still in the air
smoke causing a hazy screen
She ducks into a lane
picks up her black robe and stumbles behind a bin
Crouching, heart pounding
trying to find a way forward
She must escape, she must
She dashes across the sand
To the barbed wire fence
No matter, she'll tear her way across
to the airport, to the plane
that will take her to a place of refuge
She can almost see the beacon
Can she reach it in time?

Talisman

Words they come easy
They are my refuge, my strength
Blow away the storm

My Claim

Why do I 'need' to feel safe?
Why do I have to ask for refuge?
Why do I seek to be brave?
I am.

Who is going to grant me shelter?
Who is going to sign a guarantee?
Who appointed him there?
Not me.

Do I not have the same rights?
Do I not own the same space?
I think I do
I don't need to ask for safety
For I have it.

Sanghamitra Rath

India

Who am I?

An Architect? A Professor? Financial Planner? A blogger? Car Rallyist? Marathoner? Traveller? I have been all of these things! But I am mostly a dreamer, who loses herself in regency romances and cosy mysteries. I look forward to exploring our beautiful world more, in all its nuances.

Brave Soul

I wake up early
To see the sky is clear,
But my thoughts muddled
Morning noon evening together bundled
With too much
Pork, chicken, cream
Breakfast, lunch, dinner
A gluttony of richness
Whatsapp, Facebook, Instagram and Twitter
Netflix and Amazon Prime and Star shows
A media sensory overload
Cushions scattered; blankets huddled
Clothes scattered
Draped too much
AC, Music, Fridge
TV, Ovens, Tabs et al
Gadgets surfeit
Too much of all,
But still not enough
To feel, dream and reflect
And it is a Brave Soul
who can see the sky, clear

The Secret To Virtue

Thin and Fine
Or thick and corded
Dark and grimy or
Yellow and bright

It is a veil
It is a stole
It is a scarf
It is a fichu
It is a pallu, wimple or purdah
Mantilla, babushka, or burkha,
That guards your virtue!

A wispy piece of cloth
That's strong enough,
Stronger than wealth, wisdom,
And common sense
Oh Irony!

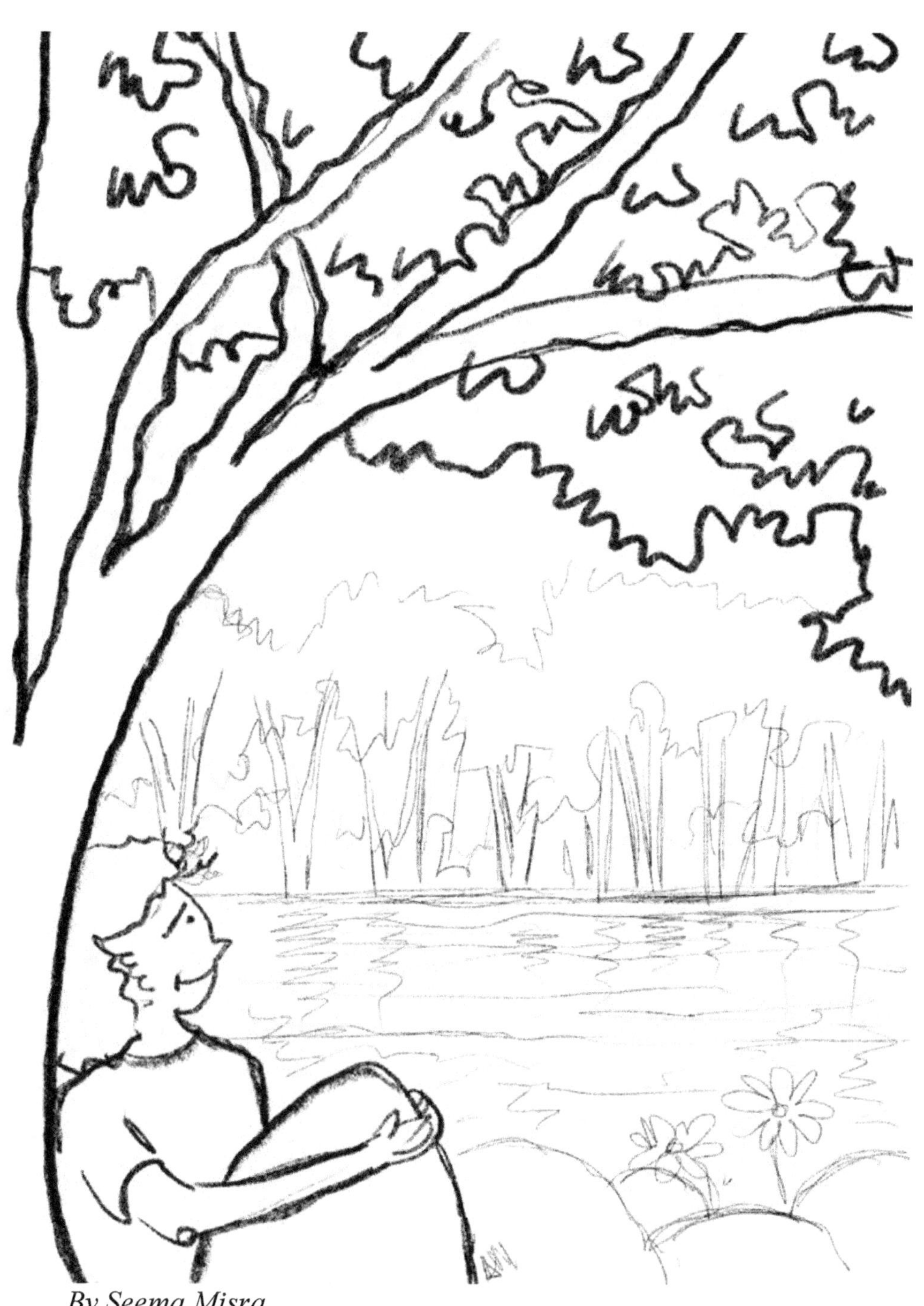

By Seema Misra

Seema Misra

A creative soul, adept with both the brush and the pen, Seema works from Bangalore, India as a communications specialist and dabbles in freelance illustration. She is happiest when sketching nature, people, food, and architecture. To unwind, she watches world cinema or travels across it! But more often than not … you will find her curled up in her favorite corner reading a book while sipping on strong coffee.

Instagram seemamisra

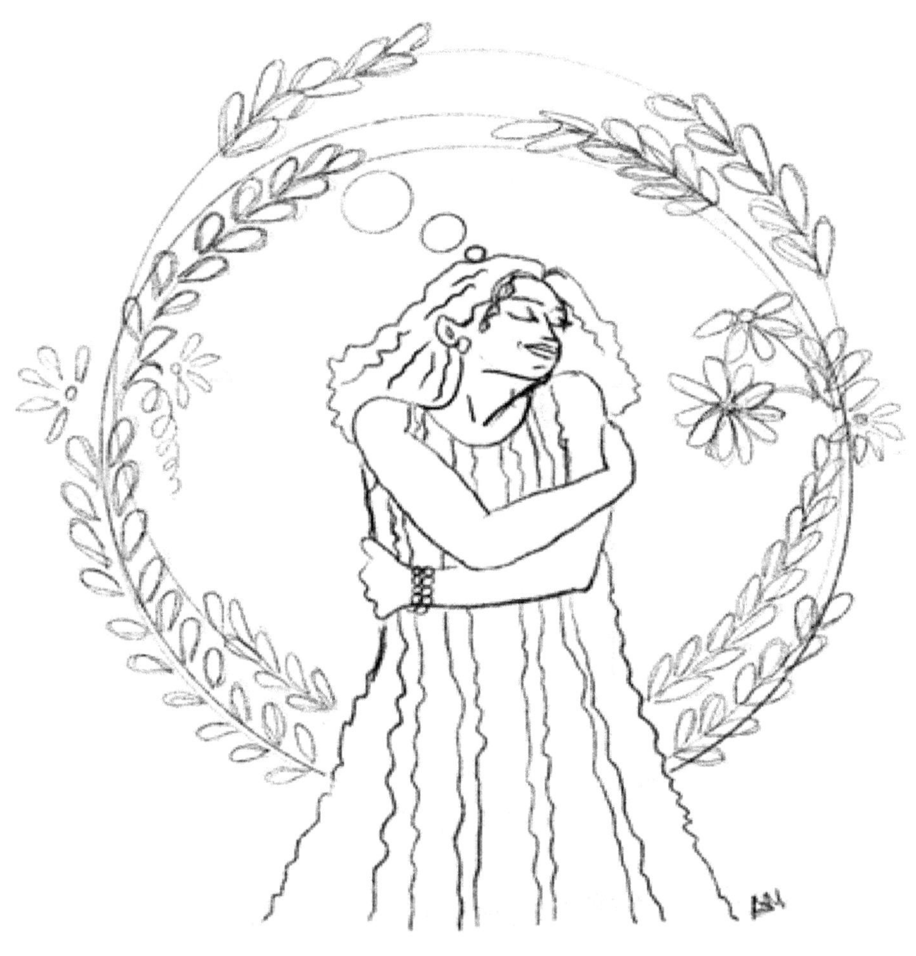

By Seema Misra

Shalu Ahuja

A flawsome techie mom, and a published children's book author, Shalu is on her journey to excavate pieces that elevate exploration and cultivate curiosity in the people she meets.

Based in India, a cultural melting pot, Shalu is boldly redefining what it means to belong - in the workplace, our families, and communities.

The Window

The birds are in their trees
readying to fly the horizon, and
the poets are at their windows,
busy making the world that soothes their soul.

Yesterday, I saw a dog chasing his tail,
the Uber driver waiting in haste, and
a chimney smoking haze.

This morning, I am staring at the wall, projecting
my childhood memories and my vision of raising two
beautiful souls -
some are clinched with anxiety to push the barricades and
some are unfolding a big window in the sky.

If there is no window opening within,
would the dreamers constantly stay outside in the Sun
or remain locked inside, staring at lifeless walls?

So, as the tapestry needle is to a weaver
and the wheel is to a potter,
the window is to the maker
for the stream of life to flow through generations.

The Lost Scarf

Once every little girl on the planet
wore a handwoven scarf,
and mine was the prettiest;
at least, I reminisce about it.

When one hatcheck girl was attending men's hats
while they fine-dined in a big glass room,
another little girl lost her scarf in a small street.

I noticed many girls searching their scarf
by knocking at each door,
asking each passing by, and
at last, throwing a sheep around their neck.

In the Baa Baa of sheep,
I felt like a silent lamb.

After my life of work,
I wish no heart ever to go cold, and
each soul filled with the warmth
lets their tears roll down the cheeks and
soak into the taught woollen scarf.

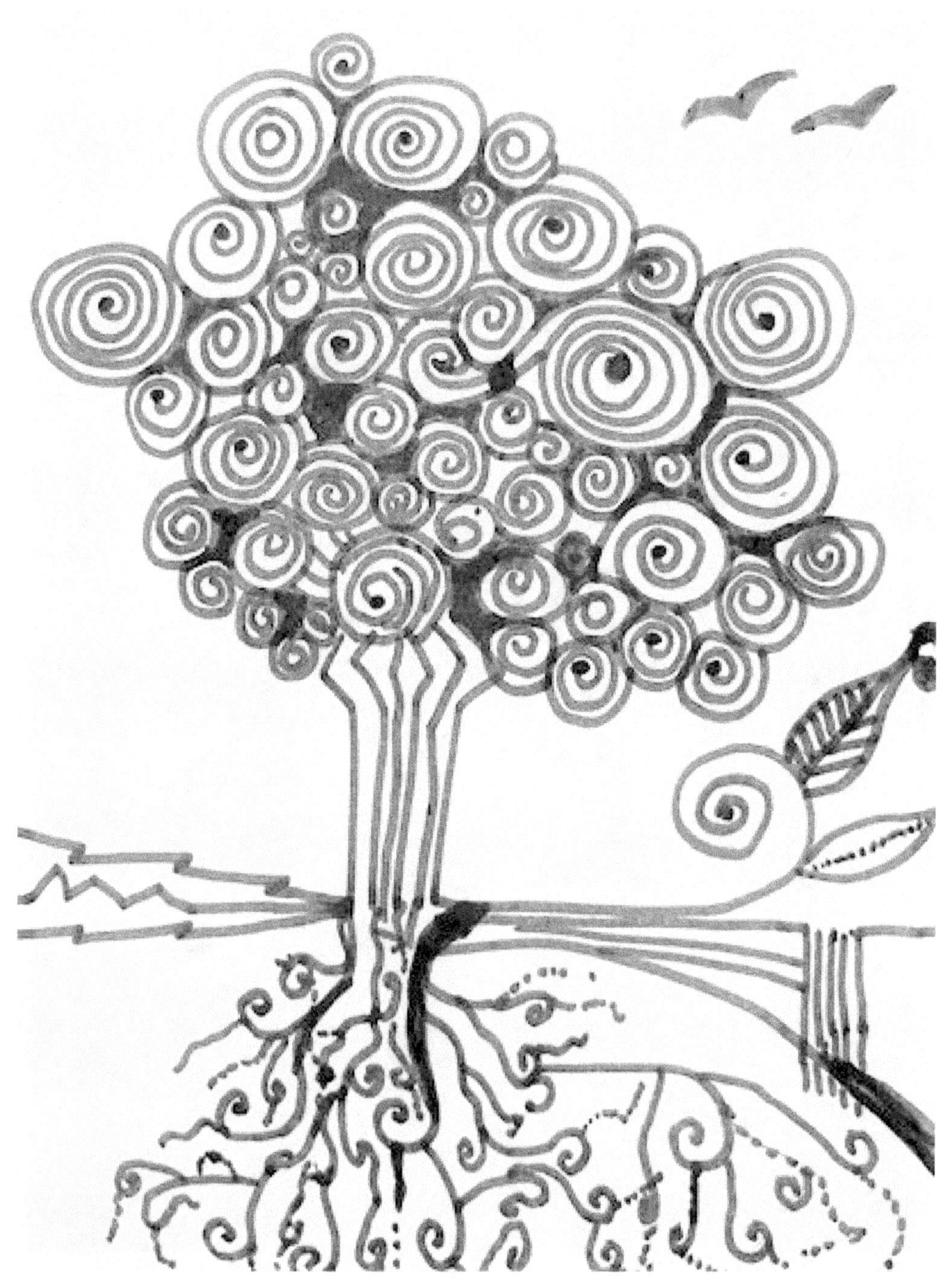

By Shalu Ahuja

Tammy Hendrix

Tammy is a fifty-eight-year-old crone; mother of two, grandmother of three, and great-grandmother of one. Forever chasing the written word, a slave to language, she strives to capture life and reality. The force behind Dreamer's Café on Facebook, she and her team work to enrich lives through poetry.

Imagination

My mind is wrought with images,
splendid reds, greens, golden hues.
Air scented of cherry blossoms, dogwood, daffodils.
Liberally blows the wind carrying my dreams along.
Free them, make of them what I have never done.

Here is where I find my aspirations,
shining like Helios riding azure skies.
I am a goddess, hair donned with daisies,
gown in regal purple flowing.
Surrounded by those who love me,
foxes, fawns, fairies dashing about in celebration.

My breast swells with joy and comfort
unlike anything I've ever known.
I escape here whenever life is too much,
dream my time away. Oh, sweet imagination
carry me abroad, grow my spirit boundless
make me what I am not.

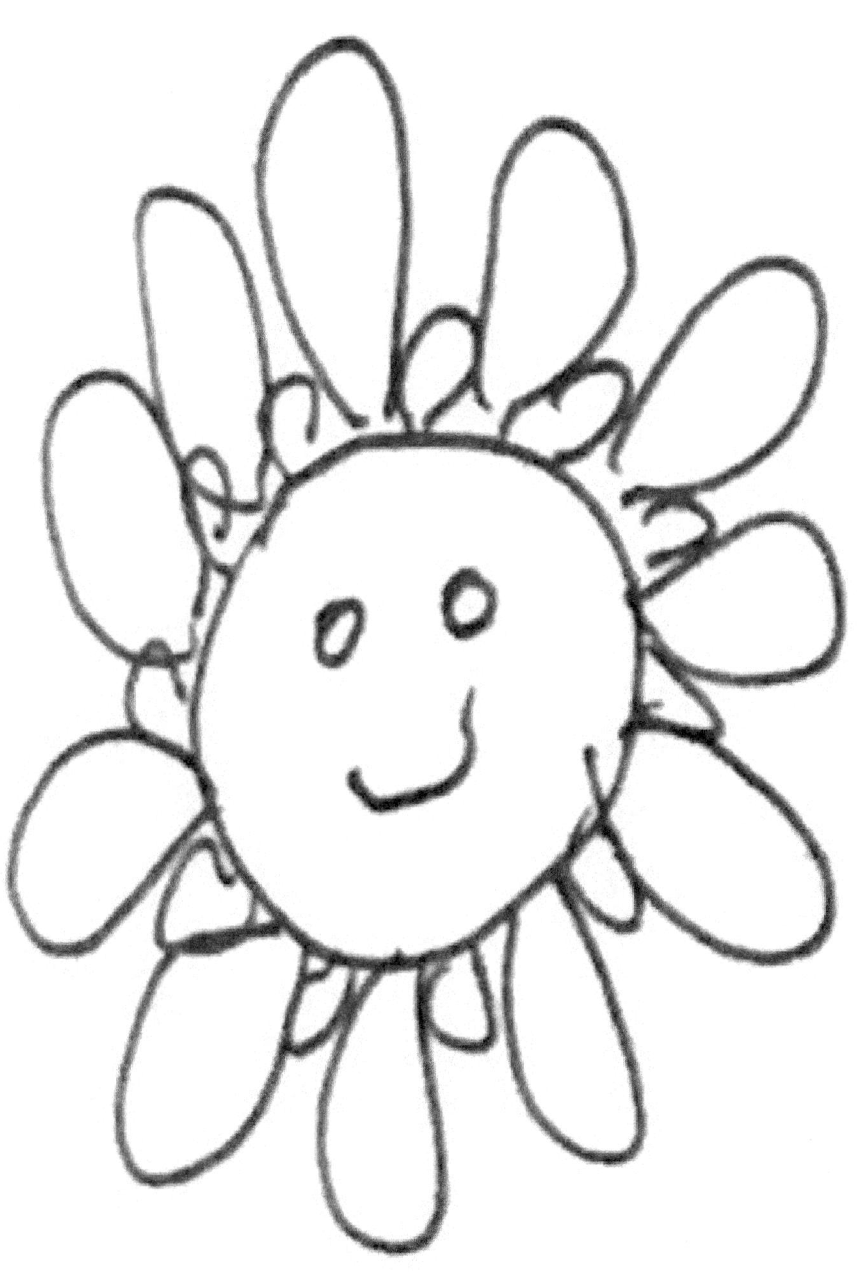

By Susan Brearley

Zaneta Varnado Johns

Zaneta Varnado Johns is a 2-time bestselling author and poet. She lives in colorful Colorado and believes that every word shared is an opportunity to love. Her poems appear in international anthologies and poetry publications. Johns is a retired human resources leader and a devoted wife, mother, and grandmother.

The Artwork (My Swing) was created from a photo. The art credit goes to my daughter, Kelli:

Kelli R. Jackson is a creative force who dismissed her middle school homework to create beautiful things. Now a full-time mother of three, this former Office Manager ensures that her children receive the creative nurturing that she craved as a child. Kelli creates visual graphics, journals, and other beautiful things.

Garden Notions

Grow your vision inside the Garden
All flowers are welcome, thorns included
Reach for a hand, flourish together
Dare to love out loud… on paper
Enter as you are… leave better
No pressure or judgement blooms here.

Opportunities exist for cross-creative germination
Find your circle… blossom where you're planted.

Nurture your intuition and muse
Engage with others—poets need other poets
Utilize all corners of this creative haven
Respect the serenity of our safe and brave space
Our inspirational calling is our sacred bond.

Covered by Prayer

When darkness looms, I retreat within my soul.
I am brave because I know what covers me—
I'm covered by the prayers of my ancestors
Prayers from Africa's Republic of Cameroon
Prayers from the bottom of the ships—
vessels that drowned dreams and freedom
in the deepest darkest depths of the ocean.
I'm covered by their incessant prayers for survival
and their woeful prayers for home.
I am covered by the prayers of tortured women and
men who landed in darkness—tormented
Prayers that cleansed their stained battered bodies
Prayers that replenished their broken spirits
Prayers that relinquished their royalty
Prayers that preserved their noble essence
Prayers that calmed unspeakable anguish
Prayers that steered them to love, despite peril
I follow the light of my resilient people
who prayed through centuries of hell
I'm covered by the prayers that brought change
Prayers that lifted us above repression
Prayers that protect me when the outside looms dark.

Joy in my Swing

Your love appears in the form of a swing
My heart's desire—your intention to bring
joy into my life, the calm I needed—
to erase stress, my dear, you succeeded.
I swing back and forth, immersed in the trees
Evergreen columns, you planted with ease
You sculpt them yearly with deliberate care
Side by side, like us—a perfect pair
Beyond the trees, God's abundance appears
Birds and windchimes, sweet sounds I hear
The grass is greener on our coveted side
Our provisions of nature reach far and wide
Faraway mountains, cottonwoods, and brush
At home in my swing, I slow my mind's rush
My swing brings peace and absolute awe
The joy I feel is tender and raw
This serene space is my personal retreat
My muse dances to my heart's happy beat
The infinite sky offers clouds galore
Magnificence surrounds me—so much to adore
I smile at the squirrels, bunnies, and flowers
Before you know it, I've been swinging for hours!

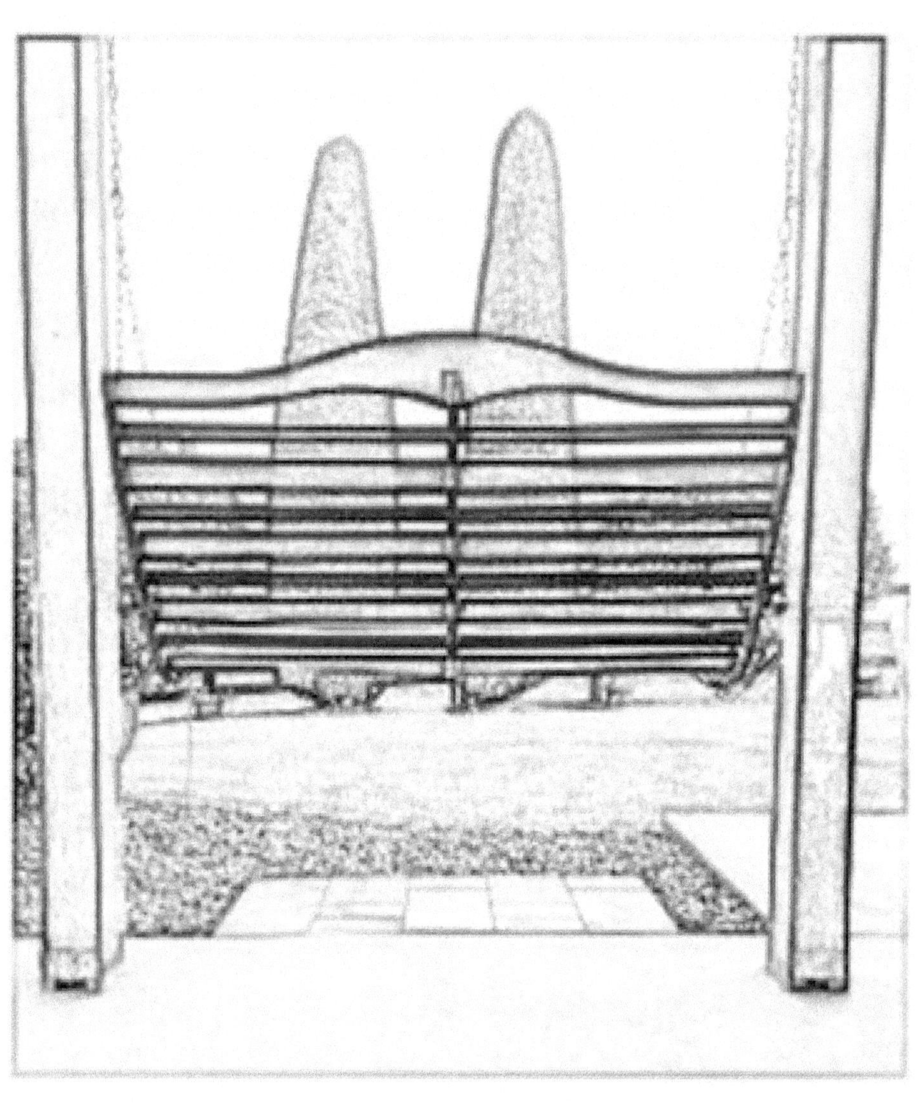

By Kelli R. Jackson

Thank you for spending your time with the Garden of Neuro poets and artists. We trust you enjoyed you journey. If you would like to explore more about the Garden of Neuro, the website is Garden of Neuro.com

We are a Safe & Brave Space for members to feel free to express themselves, expand awareness, and so much more.

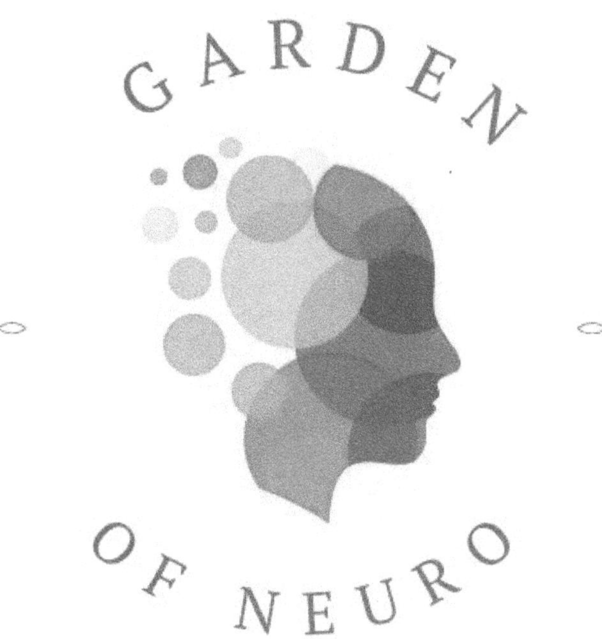

www.ingramcontent.com/pod-product-compliance
Lightning Source LLC
LaVergne TN
LVHW020631100826
845148LV00012B/2139

* 9 7 9 8 9 8 5 1 3 3 2 0 2 *